D0593950

PREACHING
FROM THE
PROPHETS

////////////////////////////////

KYLE M. YATES
Ph.D., D.D., L.L.D.

/////////

BROADMAN PRESS
NASHVILLE, TENNESSEE

PREACHING FROM THE PROPHETS

1111

4215-02

ISBN: 0-8054-1502-5

DEDICATED

to

THE YOUNG MINISTERS

who have devoted their lives to
the greatest, the most enjoyable
work in the world

PREFACE

✓✓✓✓✓✓

THE OLD TESTAMENT PROPHETS WERE PREACHERS WHO HAD color, courage and dynamic qualities. Twentieth century preachers can learn much from them. Their books will provide material for effective preaching. The truths they presented are the ones needed for this generation.

This volume has grown out of twenty years experience in the Old Testament classroom. Enthusiastic students have joined in an investigation to determine the rich preaching values which may come from the prophets. Graduate men have contributed their best efforts in this task. I have sought to arrange the material so that a busy minister or teacher or student may find in one place the help that will make it possible for him to preach or teach the truths so sorely needed in our day.

I have tried to steer clear of the critical questions and problems that come up in connection with the study of some of the prophets. It will be easy to find material on these problems in any of the good Introductions. The aim is to provide the background, the picture of the man, the contents of his book, and the messages of permanent value that may be used today. If these studies can give added power and effectiveness to the teachers and preachers of our generation they will have served their purpose.

My obligations to the world of scholars are too numerous to mention, but none the less keenly recognized and appreciated. I have been profoundly blessed by such teachers as John R. Sampey, A. R. S. Kennedy, A. C. Welch, and Philip Hitti. My constant use of the books of Bewer, Driver, G. A. Smith, Davidson, Dahl, Skinner, Robinson, Delitzsch, James, Farley, Harrell, Gordon, Leslie, Merrill, Ward, Morgan, Kirkpatrick, and Eiselen, has given me much material that cannot be properly acknowledged. If this interpretation of the prophets has any special value, it is largely due to what has been learned from my predecessors and teachers.

In the main I have tried to make an independent translation of the Scriptures used. The finished text as found in this volume is perhaps most definitely influenced by the Judson Press's special edition known as *The Holy Bible, An Improved Edition*. It is a joy to acknowledge my debt to this translation. I have also been definitely influenced by all my colleagues on the committee for the revision of the American Standard Edition.

Many of my students and some of my colleagues on the faculty of the Southern Baptist Theological Seminary have made valuable suggestions, read sections of the manuscript, checked references and encouraged me in the work.

The members of my family and the members of the Walnut Street Baptist Church have been especially helpful and sympathetic in the long months of toil. My heart goes out to all these friends in grateful acknowledgment.

KYLE M. YATES

Louisville, Kentucky, September 1, 1942

CONTENTS

CONTENTS

The Book
  Introduction
  Outline
Preaching Values
  Some great texts
  Practical lessons of permanent value

  The Times
  The Man
  The Book
  Practical Lessons of Permanent Value

  The Times
  The Man
  The Book
    The theme
    The style
    The outline
  Great Religious Ideas

  The Background
  The Man
  The Book
  Practical Lessons of Permanent Value

  The Land of Edom
  The Prophet
  The Book
    The occasion and date
    The outline
  Practical Lessons of Permanent Value

CONTENTS

INTRODUCTION

✓✓✓✓✓

THE OLD TESTAMENT PROPHETS ARE DYNAMIC FIGURES WHO speak to our age with a tremendous challenge. No set of men in all literature present a more colorful picture. The diligent student will find in them a statement of the political, social and religious conditions of the Old Testament period that he can find in no other way. These men of God give us an interpretation of history that we cannot afford to miss, and a gradually unfolding insight into the eternal purpose of God for His people.

They throw light upon our own day and our own situation by announcing the eternal principles of divine providence which will always operate whenever similar conditions are present. It is a truism to say that in God's plan the same things are true today that were true in the Old Testament age. If we are guilty of the same sins we can be sure of reaping the same punishment. It is indeed easy for us to get the word of God for our day if, capable of analyzing our own situation, we go to the prophets to find their statement of God's prescription for a similar condition.

A careful study of these men is sure to influence us to model our lives by their standards. We shall have a sterner conception of moral behavior. Color will be added to our presentation of truth. Imaginations will burn with a new activity. Recognizing the nearness of God, we will go out to take our places as active champions of the oppressed of the earth, prepared to stand alone if necessary in our loyalty to our God. Life will take on a different meaning when we realize that we are the chosen vessels of God, with an undying commitment to do His will.

A study of the gradual unfolding of the plan of God will lead us directly to Jesus Christ as the fulfillment of prophecy.

He will take His place as the King of Kings, the Lord of Lords, the great High Priest, the Suffering Servant who bore our sins in His own body on the tree. It is a marvelous study. May the Holy Spirit guide us as we journey along the way.

NAMES USED FOR THE PROPHETS

Several names were used as titles for these men who came to the people with a distinct message from God.

The word *Ro'eh,* "Seer," is used eleven times in the Old Testament to describe the spiritual forerunners of the prophets. The term indicates special powers of sight. The verb means "to see." Samuel was a seer who had attained a reputation in his community as one who was singularly successful in receiving mysterious answers from the unknown.

The word *Chozeh* is used twenty-two times in the Old Testament to denote the same idea of seeing or gazing. Balaam, Gad and some of the writing prophets are called "seers" or "gazers." The early functions of the seer merged into those of the later prophets. Both of these titles place the emphasis on the mode of receiving the truth rather than any quality of delivery or behavior.

The word *Nabhi',* found three hundred times in the Old Testament, lays stress upon the utterance of the message and not on the vision. We cannot be dogmatic about its origin but it is most probably an active noun from the old Semitic root *Naba'* "to utter, proclaim, speak." The cognate verb is found in Assyrian and Arabic with something of the same meaning. In Arabic it seems to mean the utterance of a special message on behalf of one who has commissioned him to say it. In Exodus 7:1 Moses is given Aaron as his prophet to do the speaking. Deut. 18:18, Jeremiah 1:9 and 15:19 seem to indicate that God's prophet was one qualified and called and commissioned to speak God's word to men. The English word "prophet" represents the Greek "prophetes" which indicates "one who speaks in behalf of another." The idea of prediction is present in the word throughout the Old Testament. However, the prophets were primarily speakers or preachers to their own age—witnesses as well as predictors.

The prophet was also designated by such terms as Watchman, Man of God, Servant of Yahweh, Messenger of Yahweh, Interpreter, and Man of the Spirit. Each of these terms was employed for the peculiar situation that called it forth. One of the most appropriate titles used is that of "Interpreter." Surely that was the primary task of the prophet!

THE MARKS OF A PROPHET

How are we to recognize the prophet? What are the distinguishing marks?

1. He is always an uncompromising individualist. He cannot be bound by conventions or by public opinion or be restrained by the caution of diplomats.

2. He is conscious of a divine call that holds him to the task set forth by his God. Always he must realize that he is God's mouthpiece. The divine compulsion must be obeyed.

3. He is conscious of the privilege of access to the inner counsel of Yahweh. He is in immediate contact with God. He is the bearer of precious secrets from the throne of God to needy men.

4. He is usually a man of action with a certain ruggedness of body and character that commands attention in any gathering. Being intense and keyed to a high pitch he will be apt to stir up antagonism and opposition.

5. He is conscious of God's authority and backing in all emergencies. It is usually true that he stands alone against practically all of his contemporaries. Even the religious leaders (priests and conventional prophets), who usually find time for social intercourse, are constantly challenging the strange stand of God's prophets.

6. He is very definitely a man of prayer and communion. His lonely, solitary life gives him plenty of time to keep in touch with God.

7. He is clean and consecrated in life and character. In all

the long line of genuine prophets we do not find a single breath of criticism of the moral life of any one of them. Each lived a separated life.

8. He is an outspoken critic of specific evils in the social order. Kings, priests, princes, nobles and judges are denounced fearlessly. He does not deal in abstractions. Guided by the will of God he raises his voice in violent protest against any person or institution meriting denunciation.

9. He is God's agent to reveal the future to the people. It is quite true that his main work is that of preaching to his own age. We must not, however, lose sight of the part the prophet plays in revealing the purpose of Yahweh for the future. He is given peculiar insight into the will of God for the generations yet unborn.

The Roll Call of the Prophets

It is impossible to give the exact order or to settle the precise date of these men of God who preached His message. We shall begin by listing them without estimate of the approximate date. A more detailed study of the factors determining the date will be presented later.

The Early Group

Moses	1447 or 1225	in Egypt
Samuel	1100–	in Israel
Elijah	870–	in Israel
Elisha	850–	in Israel
Joel	835– 820	in Jerusalem
Jonah	800–	in Israel

The Eighth Century Group

Amos	760–	in Israel
Hosea	745–	in Israel
Isaiah	740– 698	in Jerusalem
Micah	735–	in Jerusalem

The Seventh Century Group

Zephaniah 630– 622 in Jerusalem
Jeremiah   626– 585 in Jerusalem and Egypt
Nahum   625– 612 in Jerusalem
Habakkuk   610– 605 in Jerusalem

The Exilic Group

Obadiah 586–   in Jerusalem or Babylon
Ezekiel 592–   in Babylon

The Post-Exilic Group

Haggai   520–   in Jerusalem
Zechariah 520–   in Jerusalem
Malachi   435–   in Jerusalem

THE PSYCHOLOGY OF PROPHECY

How did the prophets get and give their messages to the people? How did God deal with them when they were transmitting messages to their hearers? How explain the trance, the dream, the ecstatic state? In the early days there was a tendency toward soothsaying, augury, clairvoyance and divination. Samuel exhibited something of the characteristics of the village clairvoyant who could solve riddles, find lost articles, pry into the unknown, and answer difficult questions. Saul, swept away by religious emotion, "prophesied among them." Elisha asked for a minstrel so that he might be in the right mood for prophecy. These are all instances of an early stage in prophecy that is completely superseded in later days. The roots of prophecy may go back to such primitive beginnings but in the golden age of Old Testament prophecy such characteristics have completely disappeared. After the days of Elijah, Hebrew prophecy became increasingly ethical and religious in its nature.

In the main we may say that these men remained normal human beings even though the consciousness of divine control exerted a strong influence upon their personalities. They were sensitive souls keenly alive to the hand of God upon them. They were conscious of a unique relationship with Yahweh that gave them direct communication with Him and a corresponding responsibility in delivering His message to all the people. Professor Sampey says: "Their mental processes were stimulated and guided by the Spirit, who clothed them with power. Imagination, memory, and reason were no doubt heightened, as well as intuition and spiritual insight. The spirit of God chose proper men for His purpose, and then turned to account all their powers. The mind of the prophet perhaps varied from the extreme of trance and ecstasy all the way to a quiet thoughtfulness over which the Holy Spirit presided. The prophets of Jehovah had little in common with dancing and howling dervishes." [1] One of the best evidences of the true prophet is that he was able to keep his consciousness and self-control while receiving and delivering his messages. It seems that Jeremiah, for example, received a great deal of his finest revelation while in possession of his normal mental consciousness. He was led by the Spirit to sense and grasp truth that was appropriate and valuable for his particular situation. Quite normally he came into possession of God's word for his hour. He certainly did not resign his consciousness.

Personality was never surrendered as the prophet received his pronouncement. He was actively alert, conscious of the needs and problems of his people. He applied himself strenuously to the task of getting the message from God. In no sense was he passively open so that, without effort, the words could flow through him, without being colored by his own mind, background and personality. It was truly the message of God to the people, but it was stated in the language of the man whom God honored with the responsibility of translating His teaching to human minds. This is clearly illustrated in the classic poetic language of Isaiah and the blunt, prosaic sentences of Micah. In each case it was the full thought of God sent to men through the medium of human personality.

[1] *Syllabus for Old Testament Study,* p. 152.

THE PRIEST AND THE PROPHET

In the religious history of the world two types of mind invariably collide: the priestly and the prophetic. The priest puts the prime emphasis on worship and finds joy in ceremonies and ritual observances. He is apt to be a conservative who finds it difficult to worship God except by means of elaborate ceremonies and liturgies. Morality has a place in his theology but it is not a prime place. Formalism becomes one of his biggest sins for religion tends to become a mere form. The prophet lays the chief emphasis on life, on conduct, on moral quality. He is constantly opposing the person who depends on mere perfunctory performance of regular duties. He irritates, prods, denounces, stands alone in his demands, insists on applying God's eternal principles to life. To him conduct is much more important than ceremonies. He is an ethical teacher, a moral reformer, a dangerous disturber of men's minds. He constantly strikes at sins, vices and lapses and seeks to stir men to holier lives.

In the New Testament Jesus took up the fight and carried it on against the scribes and Pharisees who were busy with fasts, rules, festivals and ceremonies. His emphasis was the prophetic emphasis. Men must change their lives, behave as godly creatures, put the emphasis where the prophet has always put it. He did not once call Himself a priest. When His disciples were asked to give their estimate of Him they called the names of several prophets but not a single priest. The author of Hebrews speaks of Him as a priest but quickly warns against the thought that He has any connection with the priestly group since the day of Melchizedek. When Christianity lost its power and became a priestly religion the emphasis was naturally shifted from conduct to ceremonies. The natural result came about and the church with gorgeous ritual and elaborate ceremonies became immoral and failed in its prophetic mission. This will ever be true when we fail to show concern for vital religion that issues in godly conduct.

⸺ MOSES ⸺

THE GREATEST MAN OF THE OLD TESTAMENT TIMES IS comparatively unknown to our people. A look at the facts of his life will awaken the interest of young and old. The picture of the man courageously making his way among dangers and difficulties will challenge the admiration of anyone. The significant contribution which he made to the Bible and religion certainly sets him before us as a person deserving serious attention. *There hath not arisen a prophet since in Israel like unto Moses, whom the Lord knew face to face.* (Deut. 34:10.)

THE BACKGROUND

Political conditions in the land of Egypt produced a perfect background for such a giant. The people who came into Egypt from Palestine during the days of Joseph grew into a great multitude. During the days of the Hyksos or "Shepherd Kings" they enjoyed freedom, prosperity and unlimited opportunities for happiness.

When these friendly Semitic rulers were driven out by Amosis I in 1580 B.C. a new order was established. The first great wave of anti-Semitism rolled over Israel. The native Egyptian Pharaoh sought to limit the rapid growth of these neighbors by reducing them to slavery and executing the male children. The men were used in the vast building operations. We cannot know just how long this oppression lasted. One group of scholars contends that the Exodus took place between 1290 B.C. and 1220 B.C. They would give to Rameses II, 1292-1225 B.C., the distinction of being the Pharaoh of the oppression. Another group sees in the evidence a definite date of 1447 B.C. for the date of the Exodus, in which case Thutmose III, 1501-1447 B.C., would be the ruler in the days of Israel's deliverance from slavery.

In either case it is a period of Egyptian supremacy in the world. Both the eighteenth and the nineteenth dynasties were exceptionally strong. The Tell el-Amarna letters (1375-1350 B.C.) give us many details of the political life of the world during these stirring days. In the North the Hittite empire was rapidly taking its place as a world power. In the East the Assyrians were weak but showing signs of the sort of activity that gave trouble later.

Social conditions. Moses was born in the midst of a slave community. The men of the group were forced to do hard labor in the public expansion program of the king. Living conditions could not have been good. For many years these Israelites had lived in this pastoral setting producing some food supplies, tending sheep and cattle and rearing their children. Family life was maintained with some semblance of emphasis on the early religion of the fathers. Certainly Amram and Jochebed kept their family together and gave religious instruction to the children. Fear must have entered into the minds of the mothers and fathers as they realized the inhuman methods used to prevent the increase of the male population.

In the Egyptian court, luxury and ease with an emphasis on cultural pursuits prevailed. It was an age of prosperity and plenty. Trade routes brought in wealth, luxuries and valuable supplies. Slave labor built huge structures and relieved the Egyptians of the stress of toil. Great libraries and well-equipped schools supplied the nobility with the finest advantages. The poor people and the unfortunate Israelites were oppressed.

Moses was in touch with both situations. He knew of the want, the misery, the yearnings of his own people. He was a definite part of the court life with all of its advantages, luxuries and privileges. The finest educational system of the world gave him its best. Those forty years in Egypt left an indelible mark upon him.

Religious conditions. We cannot know much about the

system of religious education in the life of the residents of Goshen. Each home was called on to provide the program of education for its children. In the home of slave people this might have been sadly neglected. However we may well believe that pious souls kept alive the fundamentals of the old faith brought to Egypt by Jacob and his descendants. When Moses began to teach them the principles of the Yahweh religion, he found that they had a basis for the great truths he was bringing. We must remember, however, that the people were woefully ignorant of the deeper things of God.

Among the Egyptians he could see a most elaborate system of religious beliefs and observances. Religion had a large place in the life and thinking of the people. Their temples were large and extravagantly furnished. Many gods vied with one another for the gifts of the multitudes who thronged the sanctuaries. On every side priests and ceremonies and religious displays met the eye. It was the golden age of Egyptian religion and Moses must have been a close student of all that passed before him.

The Man

The facts in his life. The life of Moses is easily divided into three distinct periods of forty years each.

1. IN EGYPT. Born to godly parents, adopted into the family of Pharaoh; educated in all the arts and sciences of the Egyptian universities; he makes a great choice to ally himself with his own people. Later he is forced to flee to save his life.

2. IN THE WILDERNESS. He wins a wife and a home, is subjected to the severe discipline of the desert, learns at firsthand the land through which he is to lead the people, receives the call of God to go back to Egypt for the work of his life, returns with Aaron for the task.

3. LEADING THE PEOPLE THROUGH THE WILDERNESS. He rescues the Israelites from Egypt, sees God's signal deliverance at the Red Sea, receives the *Torah* at Sinai, teaches and trains the people, loses patience and falls into sin, preaches in the plains of Moab, and is taken home to God.

The factors in his equipment for the task.

1. Early training in a godly home.
2. The influence of slavery on his young life.
3. Luxury, ease and extravagance as he learned them in the palace.
4. Firsthand knowledge of the culture, art, religion and literature of Egypt.
5. A serious defeat in an early attempt to free his people.
6. The discipline, loneliness and hard work of the wilderness.
7. The contribution of Reuel and the Kenites to his theology.
8. The rich experience with God in the solitude of the desert.
9. A thorough knowledge of the land through which he was to lead God's people.
10. The challenge of a task that would crush an ordinary man.
11. The certainty that he was God's man and that God would continue to reveal Himself to His messenger.

His personality. It will help to look carefully into all the available material so that we may be able to visualize the man Moses. What are some of the distinguishing characteristics? He was a powerful man physically, mentally and spiritually. In either realm he would excite the attention and the admiration of all who looked upon him. In a very real sense he identified himself with his people. His vigorous social passion was in evidence all through his life. He was so thoroughly unselfish that many of his acts stand forth as almost unbelievable.

His passionate devotion to Yahweh, his powerful faith in the divine plan and the divine purpose, his capacity for righteous indignation, and his spiritual intensity, mark him as a true leader of men. He was under the hand of God and his whole life was influenced by that consciousness. Even to the end of his life he sought to complete the great work which had been laid upon him. He was in such close touch with God that it was easy to know the divine will and read the clear chart of the divine purpose.

His religion. Moses certainly did not found a new religion or bring back from the desert a new God. He built upon the foundation laid in earlier days. Much that was new and valuable was received from the forty years' residence with the Kenites. Reuel and the other Kenite teachers were able to give this brilliant university student a great deal that was valuable in the forming of his theology. It is interesting to know that a man of Ur, a priest of Salem, a Balaam from the desert, a priest of the Kenites, or a teacher in Egypt, may be able to make a significant contribution to the building of a system of theology that is truly Yahweh's will for men. Melchizedek, in his own right, Reuel in his, Balaam in his, could come with a personal interpretation of the truth of the Yahweh religion. We shall never know how much the Kenites contributed to their slave cousins from Egypt. Perhaps they had preserved elements from an earlier experience that were more nearly in accord with God's gift to men.

At any rate, the religion of Moses was, in the full sense, born in a personal experience with Yahweh of Hosts in the desert of Arabia. It was a personal revelation from God to a man. It was "received" and not "created." God came to this student, who had been learning for eighty years, with the great climax to all of his study. In a divine revelation he found the elements that made up his religion. In the strength of Yahweh he took upon himself the task of leading the people of Israel to know and embrace it.

His idea of God. In the theology of Moses the thought of God's purpose for the chosen people stands out. He is a purposive God. The will of God for the world is clearly outlined. Moses is assured that he may expect a gradual unfolding of the successive steps in that purpose. He is conscious, too, that God will unfold depth upon depth of character as the days pass. It was to be an adventure through the maze with a Being who could be trusted, who knew His way, who had a clear goal toward which He was moving, "I will be what I will be."

Moses' God was a Being of moral character. Ethical standards were set up that could challenge the highest in men. God had character as well as power and He wanted His people to mirror His ethical nature.

Yahweh was a distinct personality and Moses represented Him as respecting human personality. He knew Moses face to face. He was primarily concerned with the task of producing and developing godlike personalities in the world. In speaking of the burning bush experience, Harrell says: "Jehovah became to him a real presence, speaking clearly—a righteous God, having compassion and a purpose for his people Israel. These are the contributions of Moses to revealed religion: (1) Jehovah alone is Israel's God; (2) he is a righteous being, and requires righteousness of his people; (3) he is accessible, as evidenced in particular by Israel's deliverance from Egypt and by his overshadowing providence. These are great conceptions. Analyze them, and one finds in them the root ideas of divine sovereignty, divine holiness, and divine love. These are the foundation stones on which the prophets reared the temple of faith, the pinnacle of which is Jesus of Nazareth.[1]

Here is a compassionate God who cared for His people in slavery, delivered them from bondage, led them tenderly across the wilderness, taught them by the prophet, and loved them with an undying love. He is a covenant-keeping God who has a right to expect His own chosen ones to keep their part of the covenant. Since He is Spirit He must be worshiped as a Spirit.

An estimate of the man. (Deut. 18:15-18; 34:10; Num. 12:3, 6ff.; Exod. 40:16; Heb. 11:24-28; Matt. 17:3; Luke

---

[1] *The Prophets of Israel*, p. 32. Used by permission of the publishers, The Cokesbury Press.

16:31; John 5:46; Acts 7:22; Rev. 15:3). Someone has said that "the work of the prophets is the lengthening influence of Moses." Renan says that he is "a colossus among the figures of humanity." The later prophets and authors of the Old Testament do not claim at any point to be heralds of a new doctrine. In each case they give the impression that they are champions of principles that go back to the early days of the nation's life. It is to Moses that they go for the basic principles of their religion and their theology.

Moses was the true emancipator from slavery and oppression. Under the leadership of God he performed the miracle of the ages. As a great creative personality he was able to weld into a unit people who were so oppressed that they had lost all hope. He created a national consciousness for them that made possible the elements of stability and oneness. He was for them a leader who planted the germs of truth and breathed into them a spirit that carried them through dangers, difficulties and crises. Because of his passionate devotion to Yahweh, he was able to give them an enduring religious passion that has continued to be theirs through the centuries. As a teacher of men Moses took his place with the best teachers of all time. The people spent nearly forty years in his school. They sat at the feet of one of God's greatest instructors. In the presence of such a man of prayer the people were constantly challenged to have a deeper faith in Yahweh. He was truly the prince of intercessors. His faith and unselfishness constantly rebuked the ones who knew him. He was commended especially as a meek man. This involved the inner spirit that manifested itself in the sort of life that pleased God. His will was a surrendered will. He was vitally concerned with knowing and doing the will of Yahweh. He was the most God-fearing man of his time.

His contribution as lawgiver sets him forth as one of the world's greatest men. Hammurabi had made his contribution to the law codes of the ages. Moses knew of the existing laws and was interested in their inner features. It was, however, in a unique relationship that Moses came to give to the world God's great system of laws. He was the divine representative who was inspired of God to set down the laws that God wanted His chosen people to give to the world. He was God's prophet ordained to deliver messages from the throne of God. His extraordinary achievements are explained only as we think of his call as a prophet of God. He went into the secret place with Yahweh and came back with the divine message to the hearts of men. As a prophet he was enabled to accomplish the greatest work of the Old Testament era (Deut. 34:10; Num. 12:6f.). Davidson says: "Moses found materials; but he passed a new fire through them, and by its heat welded them into unity; he breathed a spirit into the people that animated it for all time to come.[2]

Practical Lessons of Permanent Value

1. The value of early religious training in the home (Exod. 2:7-10; Deut. 6:6-9; Eccles. 12:1).
2. Necessary qualifications for leadership.
3. The futility of trying to run ahead of God (Exod. 2:11-15).
4. The extraordinary power of intercessory prayer (Exod. 32:9-14, 31, 32; 34:9; Num. 11:2; 12:13; 14:11-24; Deut. 9:12-20, 25-29).
5. Excuses anger God (Exod. 4:13, 14).
6. Men whom God places in positions of authority are held to a strict account.
7. Frequent interviews with God are necessary for power, wisdom and authority (II Cor. 3:12-18).
8. A heavenly light shines through the face of one who has been alone with God.
9. The penalty for disobedience and loss of temper is severe (Num. 20:12; 27:14).
10. When God calls a man He proceeds to qualify him.

[2] *Old Testament Prophecy*, p. 32.

11. Confidence and power come through experience and victory.

12. We are hardened for hardships by hard work.

13. The value of patience and perseverance.

14. Unbelief in God's appointed leader brings reproach on God.

15. We see ourselves as God sees us only after long hours spent alone with Him.

16. When God commands us to go forward He will lead the way.

17. Unselfishness is one of the chief marks of a great man (Deut. 9:18-20, 25-29).

18. A successful leader must love his people so much that he is willing to die for them.

19. God may take many years to prepare His chosen leader for a great task.

20. The importance of keeping alive the hope that "the bush will burn" for us. A great experience may be only a short way ahead.

··· SAMUEL ···

THE "SECOND FOUNDER" OF THE NATION ISRAEL IS A
commanding figure. Let us think of him as a toddling baby
boy discovering a world mired in ignorance, slavery, superstition and despair. Without hesitation he rolls up his sleeves
and begins tugging at the large ball in a frenzied effort to lift
it from its hopeless condition. Throughout his life he continues to exert his entire energy on that "impossible" task.
A miracle is performed and when he lays down his weary
frame the political, social and religious transformation has
taken place.

THE BACKGROUND

Political. The three hundred years from the death of Moses
to the birth of Samuel were dark for Israel. The Canaanites
did not welcome the intruders. The Philistines were especially troublesome, since they were completely in control of
much of the territory claimed by the Israelites. Yet the tribes
of Israel were not united. Each group sought to go its own
way and protect itself, if possible, while the others suffered.
Successive invasions by Syrians, Moabites, Canaanites, Mid-
ianites, Ammonites and Philistines caused havoc in the land.
In critical hours deliverers arose to help drive out the invaders and give the land temporary ease. The hand of God
was felt in these deliverances, for the people easily recognized
their own inability to cope with such overwhelming forces.
Gideon, Deborah, Jephthah, and Samson were used to overthrow great hordes of men who had taken possession of the
land of Israel.

In Egypt the twenty-first dynasty was just coming to the
throne after the weak twentieth dynasty had failed completely. The golden days of power and influence were gone
forever from the land of Egypt. In Assyria Tiglath Pileser I

(1120-1090 B.C.) had built up a mighty kingdom but did not come in contact with the struggling people of Israel. The Hittite empire was in decay by that time but the Aramean kingdom was rapidly becoming a troublesome power.

Social. Complex situations confronted the people in the new land. The years of conquest and possession had introduced them to uncounted social problems. They were called upon to adjust themselves to new and trying conditions. During the period of the Judges the situation had been serious. Constant oppression and frequent wars did their part to keep the people unsettled and to grind them under the wheels of poverty. No settled government could be counted on to weld them together in a solid front against the powerful enemies. When Samuel came upon the scene the Philistines had reduced them to abject slavery. They were even deprived of means of sharpening their farm tools. It was a tragic hour in Israel.

Religious. It is difficult to visualize a people without preachers and definite religious instruction for three hundred years, yet very few representatives of God appeared. In addition to this picture, it will be necessary to see encircling the people a ring of neighbors with their idols, their gods, their heathen rites, cults, customs and ceremonies. Along with these practices went certain immoral conceptions and low moral standards that produced a type of life that was not at all conducive to spiritual worship.

The central sanctuary was at Shiloh where the ark was kept and the high priest of the land officiated at the sacred altar. Eli was the grand old man of Israel when Samuel was born. Evidently he did the best he could with a bad situation, although his sons proved a real barrier to spiritual religion by desecrating the sacred place and causing the people to lose their respect for priestly authority.

Throughout the land there were bands of young men who exhibited a definite passion for religion. These "prophets" were seeking truth and a fuller expression of their deep religious desires. How they needed a strong soul to lead them into a higher understanding of God and His purposes for His chosen people!

The Man

His equipment. Samuel came into the world with a remarkable possession that was more valuable than words could tell. His mother was a godly woman and had spent years in agonizing prayer for the boy. What a blessing it was to start life with such an advantage! The influence of the godly home with earnest prayers of thanksgiving made a real contribution in the building of the man. The solemn dedication at the sanctuary, when the mother literally gave him to the Lord as a votive offering, entered into the fuller development of God's future leader. The visits year by year when Hannah came to see her son strengthened the impressions already made in his tender years.

The importance of the training in the sanctuary under Eli, the priest, can hardly be exaggerated. Eli failed with his own boys but his work with the young Samuel bore fruit. Those quiet years in the sacred precincts under the hush of Eli's presence did much to prepare the boy for God's work.

The mysterious call from Yahweh came into the young life in such a manner and with such force that he could never be the same again. That experience was epoch-making in its importance. The boy was convinced that he was actually hearing the voice of Yahweh Himself. It dawned upon him that God was depending on him for future achievements. His ears would be the ones to receive divine messages for the people. He must be ready to hear God's words and put them into action. Throughout his long life he continued to grow into a fuller realization of God's purpose for his life.

His work. Samuel was God's man for one of the darkest hours of Israel's life, a crisis of serious nature. As a seer he established himself in the kingdom as the one genuine representative with whom God was working. As a priest he succeeded to the high office made sacred by Aaron, and had the privilege of representing the people in sacrifice to God. As a leader of the people he quickly took his place to save the land from the dreaded assaults of the hated Philistines. He actually freed the people from slavery and gave them a national existence. They were drawn together under the terrific pounding of the enemy to rally around this vigorous new leader. As a judge he exercised a mild rule over them and visited various centers for encouragement and for the settling of disputes. He was the recognized authority among them even though he constantly insisted that they were in a theocracy and that God should be their Ruler. As a maker of kings Samuel took a high place. Both Saul and David were chosen and anointed during the active days of the great old man. As a man of prayer he demonstrated his power with God. The people depended on him to do the praying for the kingdom. Jeremiah gave him an outstanding place among the world's greatest intercessors (Jer. 15:1).

As a prophet of Yahweh Samuel was greatest. These other qualities and positions were possible because he was primarily God's messenger. He was honored with a divine call that gave to him special revelations for the people that could come in no other way. He was the mouthpiece of God in an hour of dire need. Then as a teacher of men he took high rank. All the people needed his teaching but the sons of the prophets were the ones through whom his best contribution bore fruit. His activities in the field of theological education will always stamp him as a great servant of Yahweh. Leslie says: "It was at this point that Samuel made a great contribution. He had the wisdom not to oppose this wild ecstasy, but to utilize it, give it guidance (I Sam. 19:20), and link it to great Israelite objectives. Under his hands it became an expression of devotion to Yahweh and a fountain of nationalistic enthusiasm." [1]

James says: "Samuel marks a fresh beginning in Israel. He

[1] *Old Testament Religion*, p. 118. Used by permission of the publishers. The Abingdon Press

is the first great man of God since Moses. He is the second of the mountain peaks that tower above the nation's history, forming a mighty range from Moses to Christ. When he died Israel was on its way to a better future. There was about him an austere purity, an uncompromising simplicity and directness, a lofty way of looking at life, a sinking of self in the good of his people, a burning desire for Israel's welfare, a passionate advocacy of its cause before God, a faith, a perseverance, a continuance in service, a willingness in his old age to meet a new situation and to throw himself whole-heartedly into the support of a younger man—that rank him with the chiefest of those men of God who were Israel's unique gift to the world." [2]

His character. Samuel was deeply religious. From his early childhood experiences he became conscious of God in his life and showed evidences of this on many occasions. He was obedient to Yahweh and to Eli. That trait of character continued throughout his long life. He had the qualities that made God choose him from among all the boys of his generation to rise to that high station. When God selects one from such a multitude it is quite clear that there are some definite qualities that stand out. He was magnanimous in his thought and acts. His personal life was above reproach. Watch the old man as he calls the people together and challenges them to point out a single act of dishonesty or selfishness in his long life. A man of outstanding integrity, he could stand the gaze of the crowd without flinching. He had a burning social passion that kept him active in helping his people. Throughout his long life he spent himself. He literally carried the nation on his heart.

PRACTICAL LESSONS OF PERMANENT VALUE

1. What a work one man can do when God controls and directs him!

---

[2] *Personalities of the Old Testament,* pp. 94, 95. Used by permission of the publishers, Charles Scribner's Sons.

2. Personal piety can never be a substitute for parental discipline.

3. It is good to listen for the voice of God.

4. It is just as essential to answer when He calls.

5. Obedience is better than sacrifice (15:22).

6. The value of early religious training in a godly home.

7. The happy state of the man who has lived a life above reproach in every detail.

8. God is never satisfied with partial obedience.

9. A true servant of God may be called upon to train a younger man who will overshadow him in the estimation of the people.

10. It is not necessary for one to withdraw from political life in order to exert spiritual leadership.

11. Compromise with evil is expensive and deadly.

12. God can only use men who are willing to be used and only so far as they will let Him use them.

13. A child has no trouble hearing the voice of God when he has been conceived in prayer and reared in the house of God.

''' ELIJAH '''

In Jewish tradition the prophet Elijah takes first rank. Through all the years he has continued to hold his high place as one of the truly great men of Israel. His life is filled with interesting adventures that urge the imagination to run riot. Such color calls for a careful study of the man, his age, his contemporaries, his message and his influence.

The Background

Political. After the death of Samuel the newly formed kingdom of Israel suffered severely at the hands of the Philistines. Their greatest invasion resulted in the death of Saul and his son Jonathan. David came to the throne of the tribe of Judah for a few years and then was elevated to be king over all Israel. Solomon followed him in a long and prosperous reign. Wealth, luxury, foreign cults and fashions were brought in. The kingdom was enlarged to include a greater part of Palestine.

In 931 B.C. the division came. Rehoboam, failing in a crisis, was left with the smaller of two adjacent kingdoms. In the North Jeroboam led the people into idolatry and pagan worship. After fifty years of disaster and turmoil Omri came to the head of the government to stop anarchy, conquer Moab, establish a monarchy, build the city of Samaria, make a treaty with Syria, and marry his son Ahab to the daughter of Ethbaal of Tyre. Omri was one of the strongest rulers of the entire lot. During this period in the land of Moab, Mesha ruled over a powerful kingdom. The famous Moabite Stone was set up to commemorate the deliverance from Israel.

Ahab, the successor to Omri, might have been more popular and famous if he could have lived apart from the influence of Jezebel. The sacred historian did not see some of the finer things which he did because of his close affinity with Baalism and other heathen religions.

Jezebel, the daughter of the priest of Melkart, was a powerful figure. She was a passionate missionary who sought by all means available to make her religion dominant in the land. Under her vigorous leadership a real crisis arose. It was a genuine life-and-death struggle. Not only did she build her own temple and import hundreds of her own alien prophets but she set out to cut off all the prophets of Yahweh and turn the people away from Yahweh worship.

Assyria began to show signs of life during this period after years of comparative quiet. In the year 854 B.C. Shalmanezer III of Assyria came against the people of Palestine. The battle of Karkar settled the fate of the Westland for many years. Ahab had an army in that battle.

In Judah (the southern kingdom) Rehoboam, Abijah and Asa ruled over the remnant of David's domain. Two serious invasions from the south by Shishak and Zerah proved serious blows to the struggling kingdom. Jehoshaphat, who was king in Jerusalem during Elijah's ministry, did much to restore some of the glory of David's reign.

Social. The land of Israel suffered greatly during the days of anarchy and invasion. As a result of the tragic turmoil of those days, living conditions were intolerable. Omri put an end to the internal disturbances but was forced to fight surrounding nations. In his vast building operations at Samaria it was necessary for him to force his people to give of their time and labor and resources until a duplicate of Solomon's dilemma must have faced him. A severe drought added to the want, the misery and the suffering of the people. While the king's court was able to maintain luxury and extravagance, the people slaved.

Jezebel, with her imported priests and prophets, introduced a new element into the life of the people. It was quite an undertaking to support these men and their elaborate worship program. A more serious matter, however, grew out of Jezebel's conception of property rights. She had no scruples whatever about the execution of a property owner and the confiscation of the land for her own desires. Fear, hatred, distrust and active disloyalty created a serious state of affairs in the kingdom. The work started by Omri was largely ruined by the coming of this Tyrian princess.

Religious. Elijah stood in the midst of a serious crisis in Israel. The people had lost practically all the finer appreciation of the Law and the principles of religion enunciated by Moses and Samuel. They had learned to know the gods of the surrounding peoples and had gradually adopted toward them an attitude of toleration that bordered dangerously on syncretism.

The marriage of Ahab to Jezebel was the fatal blow that introduced into Israel the cult which threatened to destroy the very existence of the Yahweh religion. Jezebel was not content to allow her religion to have a small place in the capital city (as the foreign wives of Solomon had done) but set about to accomplish the utter extermination of prophets and principles. Farley says: "To please his strong-minded queen, Ahab built in Samaria a temple to 'the Baal,' and also made 'the Asherah,' so that the Phoenician worship was now established in its entirety. The Baal worship was essentially the worship of mere power—of power as distinguished from righteousness—and the worship of power by a regular and logical process becomes literally the worship of evil. Not without reason did the Jews of later days designate this Tyrian deity the 'Prince of Devils.' " [1]

Along with these practices came the most hideous immorality imaginable. Moral standards were lowered and the religious life of the people fell to an alarming state. The prophets of Yahweh were persecuted. Many of them were killed. Others were compelled to hide in caves and holes or were soon silenced. The great mass of the people were "limp

[1] *The Progress of Prophecy*, p. 36. Used by permission of the publishers, Fleming H. Revell Co.

ing" along unable to distinguish between Baal and Yahweh. It was a dark day for the true religion. The leaven of Baal was working secretly throughout the entire land.

THE MAN

Facts in his life. We take it for granted that Elijah was born and bred in Gilead on the east side of the Jordan. The following brief outline sums up his ministry:

1. Appearance at the court of Ahab announcing the long drought to be broken only by God's word through the prophet.
2. Fed by the ravens at the Brook Cherith.
3. At Zarephath in Phoenicia he is cared for in the home of the widow. He restores the son to life.
4. Meets Obadiah and Ahab.
5. The contest on Mount Carmel. God answers by fire; the prophets of Baal are killed and rain comes in answer to Elijah's prayer.
6. The threat of Jezebel sends him away on a long run to the South Country.
7. The "juniper tree" experience.
8. At Horeb, the mount of God. He is stilled by the wind, the earthquake and the fire, and hears the challenge of God to return to anoint Hazael, Jehu, and Elisha.
9. The calling of Elisha to be a prophet.
10. The denunciation of Ahab in the vineyard of Naboth.
11. Quiet years as a teacher of young men who are to carry on the prophetic work.
12. His translation while Elisha looks on and receives the commission to carry on the great work.

His character. Elijah was a sturdy, virile, daring man from the wilds of Gilead. His iron constitution, his austere spirit, his majestic bearing, his flaming indignation, his consuming zeal, and his courageous nature set him forth as a man of mystery and romance. He was so strong and yet so weak. His zeal was as limitless as his energy. His tremendous grip on God gave him unusual power in prayer. His faith in God was so strong that it beggars description. He hated false religions, pagan practices and ungodly treatment of the people's rights. In most instances he displayed a remarkable unselfishness and an utter disregard of personal safety. He was merciless and cruel in his treatment of the prophets of Baal when circumstances demanded a complete victory. Literally on fire for God, he gladly burned himself out doing the will of God.

His contribution. He was Yahweh's champion in a dark day of crisis when true religion was practically driven from the earth. The people could not serve two gods. They were challenged to choose between Yahweh and the Tyrian Baal. It was his task to deal the deathblow to Baal in the land of Israel.

Just as truly was he a champion of the people in their fight against Jezebel's dictatorship. The ancient laws of property were the true foundation of the people's rights. Yahweh was revealed as the God of fair play. Righteousness was the ruling attribute of the God of Elijah. Religion and morality were closely blended in his religion. He set forth justice as an elemental requirement. No generation will ever forget the tragic story of Naboth's vineyard and Elijah's flaming denunciation of the sin of Ahab and Jezebel.

He was a teacher of Elisha and the other young men of the "schools of the prophets." These years of quiet work with his religious successors bore rich fruit. It is difficult to evaluate the contribution of one who transmits to his pupils the store of spiritual knowledge gained through his long years of study. Elijah gave to Elisha the knowledge, the vision, the challenge to serve, and the courage to finish the work begun so dramatically.

An estimate of the man. In some strange way Elijah has taken his place in the literature of the world and in men's thoughts as a truly remarkable character. The New Testament has more reference to him than to any other prophet.

At every passover the Jews look for him and keep an extra chair for his use. Mountains are named for him in Greece. The order of Barefooted Carmelites in the Roman church looks back to Elijah as its founder.

He was a man of God. Always there was about him something of the divine presence. When men saw him they were awed by the realization that God's man was in their midst.

He was a man of prevailing prayer. Where else do we find such a mighty man of prayer? The two instances of his praying on Mount Carmel literally lift him out of the ordinary into the sublime.

He was a man of faith. His unwavering faith in Yahweh made it possible for him to prevail in prayer and to continue the relentless fight against false religions and pagan behavior. Step by step he moved under the guidance and protection of his God.

In that desperate hour of crisis he was the human agent whom God used to pull the tottering theocracy back from seeming defeat. One shudders to think of the narrow escape. God's man was put forward, clothed with supernatural power, to undertake the impossible, that the divine purpose might be fulfilled.

Leslie says of him: "He was one of the most dynamic personalities in Israel's religious history, and the dramatic unexpectedness of his appearances and exits is in perfect accord with the volcanic quality of his spirit. As Sellin says: 'He went through history like a meteor.' " [2]

Ward says: "There is no more romantic figure in the Old Testament than Elijah, the Tishbite. He stands before us like a great mountain peak. There is something majestic and awe-inspiring, in the solitude that marked his life, and in the way he dominated the day in which he lived." [3]

Farley says: "Was there ever a mere man from whose life

[2] *Ibid.*, p. 145.
[3] *Portraits of the Prophets*, p. 11. Used by permission of the publishers, Richard R. Smith. Inc.

we might derive deeper encouragement in this world of conflict, where every man has his battle to fight? Elijah's courage, face to face with 'wickedness in high places'; his faith, in presence of seeming impossibilities; his prayerfulness, strong and persistent, when the heavens were as brass; his human weakness, lifted into strength by the touch of Divine compassion; above all—the great truth, as true for us as for Elijah, that all life is surrounded by grand spiritual forces." [4]

Taylor says: "The courage of Luther, the plainness of speech of Latimer, the devoutness of Calvin, and the perfervid impetuosity of Knox, were all united in the character of this man of God." [5]

Cadman says: "A hieratic grandeur overspread his monumental figure. He seemed to gather into himself those loftier hopes which have made his memory affluent for good among Jews and Christians alike. He needed neither tomb nor epitaph to perpetuate a name than which no braver glows in the golden roll of Israel's prophets." [6]

Harrell says: "Like a storm on a midsummer afternoon which by sudden stroke clears the sultry atmosphere, the thunderous Elijah, by bold, decisive action, saved his people from the encroachments of Canaanite paganism." [7]

Macartney says: "He was one of those few men 'of whom the world was not worthy.' That such a man lived makes us rejoice in our common humanity. As eloquent Wendell Phillips said over the grave of John Brown, 'Men will believe more firmly in virtue now that such a man has lived and died.' Carmel itself was not more rugged and more majestic than that prophet when he stood upon the mountain peak, his face flushed with the splendid victory over the howling priests of Baal." [8]

[4] *Ibid.*, pp. 39, 40.
[5] *Elijah*, p. 35.
[6] *The Prophets of Israel*, p. 27. Used by permission of the publishers. The MacMillan Company.
[7] *Ibid.*, p. 37.
[8] *Wrestlers with God*, p. 119.

Wiener says: "Elijah met the danger of the submersion of the nation by the Phoenician religion single-handed. Without him all Israel must have abandoned the faith which alone preserved the nationality and those great principles without which the nationality would be worthless." [9]

PRACTICAL LESSONS OF PERMANENT VALUE

1. All life is surrounded by spiritual forces.
2. Prevailing prayer settles issues.
3. Human life, human rights, and the right to property are sacred possessions.
4. National righteousness is far more important than national power.
5. No man who stands for right stands alone.
6. God does not discard us when we run away but He finds a way to revitalize and use us.
7. Sufficient physical rest and nourishment are required if we are to know and understand God's will.
8. One Spirit-filled man may change the destiny of a nation.
9. "Vales of trouble are separated from mountains of triumph by a few moments of prayer."
10. One is fitted for his life work by seasons of quiet meditation and waiting on God.
11. God's man may be certain of the presence of God in all the dark experiences of life.
12. The highest form of obedience is to continue to remain at our post of duty when we cannot see why we are kept there.
13. "Trouble reveals need and need impels prayer."
14. God's mercies and deliverances give us new faith and confidence for future crises.
15. God is gentle and tender in dealing with one who is discouraged and despondent.

⁹ *The Prophets of Israel,* p. 151.

16. The tonic of a new task is still God's way of restoring drooping spirits.
17. God always has His man ready in the hour of emergency.
18. God finds use for each of the distinct individualities of His servants (Elijah, Elisha, Peter, Paul, John).
19. The tremendous value of one man who is wholly committed to God.

⟨⟨⟨ AMOS ⟩⟩⟩

In a day when both society and religion were bankrupt, a strange personality emerged from the Judean wilderness to burn the message of God upon the minds of the people of Israel. What a terrific arraignment he delivered! How it withered all who heard it! We should know this man Amos and understand the conditions that called him forth. We want to know the contemporaries who influenced him, and those who were influenced by him. The younger prophets, Hosea, Isaiah and Micah received their impetus from this early champion of Yahweh.

The Background

Historical and political. Since the days of 854 B.C. Assyria had shown a growing interest in Palestine. In the campaign of that year Ahab had joined with other smaller states to stem the tide of an Assyrian invasion led by Shalmaneser III. After a rather indecisive battle at Karkar the Assyrians re-tired to remain in the background for several years.

From the accession of Jehu in 842 B.C. the people of Israel were subjected to fierce treatment at the hands of Syria. Hazael, taking advantage of Assyria's weakness, succeeded in keeping the Israelites in subjection. When, however, Adad-nirari III became king of Assyria he smashed Damascus in one vigorous campaign. The supremacy of Syria was ended. This signal deliverance left Jehoash and the Israelites free to breathe again. It was now an easy matter to drive out the Syrian garrisons and to make the borders safe from attack. Since the Assyrians were not able to follow up their victory and sweep on into Palestine Jehoash found time to begin building a great kingdom. Not until the coming of Tiglath Pileser (745-727 B.C.) was the land troubled by another invasion. Thus from 805 B.C. to 740 B.C. the land of Israel enjoyed a season of peace and tranquillity. The surrounding nations did not have sufficient strength to give her trouble.

Jeroboam II came to the throne in 783 B.C. and began a vigorous building program. He easily recaptured the lost territory and extended the limits of his kingdom from the entering in at Hamath to the brook of the Arabah. It would be difficult to exaggerate the significance of the military exploits of Jeroboam.

Uzziah built along the same lines in the South. Judah was made into a strong, vigorous kingdom with armies, fortifications, trade routes and powerful political alliances. These two aggressive kings carried their small kingdoms along in the same stride from victory to victory. The old limits of the kingdom built by David and Solomon were reached. It was a period of expansion, freedom, activity, prosperity and peace. Money poured in; the armies were always victorious. The people were filled with a pride in their armies and their accomplishments. No one had any anxiety or fear of invasion. They could not imagine that the powerful Assyrian empire would return after a temporary lull. Nothing interfered to chill the popular spirits. It is always tragic to watch a nation in its supreme moment of success and realize that it is but the prelude to the hour of darkest doom.

From the title (1:1) and from 7:10, 11 we know that both Uzziah and Jeroboam II were on the throne when Amos came to Israel to preach. Knowing that Jotham was actually the ruler during the last fourteen years of Uzziah's life we are led to limit the possible years for the ministry of Amos to the years 780-752 B.C. The successes and triumphs that gave Israel the freedom, the luxury, and the ease that led to its advanced state of social collapse must have taken a number of years. It is evident then that Amos must have appeared during the closing days of the period—perhaps between 760 and 750 B.C. Isaiah and Micah were young men in Judah. Hosea was alive in the Northern Kingdom. Tiglath Pileser was a growing youth with dreams of world conquest. Zechariah in Israel and the weak Ahaz in Judah were probably quite young. The great old preacher, Jonah, might still have been alive when Amos began his ministry.

Social Conditions. We find in the book of Amos a vivid picture of the social conditions of Israel at the time. It was a period of unprecedented prosperity. Wealth abounded and the people gave themselves over to a life of luxury and self-indulgence. Winter houses and summer houses with plenty of hewn stone and ivory paneling were found among the wealthy citizens. Business was good, wine was plentiful, ivory couches and rich furnishings were provided along with delicacies and stirring music for the feasts and banquets. Ease and extravagance contrasted with the misery and suffering of the slave population who could not afford the bare necessities of life. There were plenty of palaces and also plenty of hovels. The cities were growing. The merchant class made the money and took possession of the land until the most of the land was concentrated in the hands of a few. The judges were dishonest; the government was corrupt. Usury, extortion, riots, and class hatreds were visible on every hand. Along with all of this was found a shallow optimism that seemed utterly oblivious to the tragic certainties just around the corner.

The rich gained their wealth by injustice and oppression. The poor workers in the fields suffered at the hands of the cruel landowners and the heartless creditors. The dishonest merchants and venal judges conspired to make the lives of the poor miserable beyond endurance. None of these wealthy ones seemed to have concern for the sufferers. The women of the land, as heartless as their husbands, made such demands on their men that they, in turn, heaped new burdens upon the peasants (4:1). It was a dark hour in the life of God's chosen nation.

Religious conditions. The people were outwardly religious. Great numbers made journeys to the shrines at Bethel Gilgal and Beersheba. Songs, offerings, church attendance, elaborate ceremonies, and regular religious observances were all visible in abundance. The people were very pious in their claims to be the special creatures of Yahweh. There was much eschatological expectation. They longed for the Day of Yahweh.

Unfortunately, however, their particular brand of religion did not make for better moral behavior. Their religious leaders were professional preachers. Immorality was rife, the righteous were hated and opposed, there was much insincerity and cant and superstition in the sort of ritual they called worship. Gross immorality was openly aided and abetted by the religious leaders.

The rich nobles who took the lead in religious matters were selfishly indifferent to the cries and groans of a suffering multitude who suffered because of injustice, oppression and violence. These men were incapable of seeing the inner flaws which the keen eyes of Amos could see so clearly. They did not know God. They were utterly lacking in the knowledge that would let them understand the true nature of religion. Instead of plain living they knew drunkenness, extravagant meals, carousals, lolling on soft couches, idling away precious time while swift retribution made its way toward them.

The Man of God

This simple country preacher left his home in Judah and journeyed twenty-two miles to Bethel in the Northern Kingdom as God's messenger to his neighbors in Israel.

His home. Tekoa was a small village about twelve miles south of Jerusalem bounded by limestone hills and wilderness stretches. The Dead Sea, in plain view some four thousand feet below, was about eighteen miles away. It was a wild, desolate, deserted spot. The lonely hills provided the atmosphere for the training of God's prophet.

His equipment. One wonders just how Amos came to have such a remarkable grasp of world problems and their solution. He knew the world about him. In an intimate way he

could put his finger on the exact sin of each of the surrounding nations. He knew the sins of Israel as accurately as if he
had spent all his days in special detective work in Samaria.
He knew in detail the background and early history of Philistia, Syria, Judah and Israel. The laws, traditions, sins, failures
and triumphs of Israel's past life were not only clear to him
but he took it for granted that the people also knew them.
He shows some knowledge of astronomy. All this helped him
interpret God's will for the people in an exceptional way.

His training. The wilderness life gave to a strong man
like Amos just the training needed to equip him for the most
effective ministry. The solitude, the loneliness, the glory of
God in nature, the silent communion with God, the mental
concentration, the prolonged meditation on great thoughts,
the hardships, the inspiration from great natural scenes, the
contacts with traders and travelers, combined with his natural gifts to produce a rare specimen of manhood. Surely God
built a mighty man when He needed a prophet to speak in
Bethel. The travels to wool markets, the constant care of the
sheep, the extra work in pinching sycamore buds, and the
hours of conversation with merchants who traveled between
Egypt and the East, gave to this alert mind the essential
elements in his education. His major course was in theology.
How intimately he came to know God! How strong and deep
were his convictions! How perfectly he understood the religion of the Spirit! How clearly he saw through the weak,
helpless, useless sort of religion that passed as genuine in
Israel!

His call. We do not know much about the manner of the
call. He was not a member of the prophetic group. His time
had not been spent in a divinity school. He was unwilling to
be classed as a member of the guilds who made their living
by bowing to the wishes of the people and preaching a pleasing message that would guarantee a return engagement.

He was pulled away from his sheep in the wilderness by
a tremendous conviction that God wanted him to preach to

the people at Bethel. It must have been a profound experience with the Almighty in the desert that left such an indelible impression on the herdsman. The hand of God was upon him. He could not hold back.

> *And Yahweh took me from after the flock; and Yahweh said to me, Go, prophesy to my people Israel.*

It was an imperious challenge that could not be denied. Nothing short of instant obedience could please his God.

His mission. Why should he be sent to Bethel? Surely Jerusalem needed the message. Nevertheless God wanted the people of the Northern Kingdom to have a strong word of warning. Bethel was a small town ten miles north of Jerusalem. It was the seat of the chief national sanctuary where Jeroboam II worshiped. God directed the messenger to that spot where all the forces were converging to break down the true worship of Yahweh. Materialism, luxury, ease, drinking, bribery, extortion, shallow thinking and actual immorality were proving too much for the weak religious foundations. Amos was sent to people who felt no need for preaching. They lacked the necessary basis for a true understanding of a spiritual message. He was called to do his best to get a hearing and to drive home truths that God was directing against them.

His personal life. Born and bred in the wilderness, Amos had a hard life. Tending sheep and caring for the unpalatable sycamore buds constituted the work of poor peasants. His daily activities among the solitary wastes continued over a period of many years. His trips to the trade centers gave him the sort of contacts that broke the monotony for him and gave him an intimate knowledge of the peoples of the world.

When God laid hands on him for missionary activity it was necessary for him to turn away from his regular duties and go by way of Jerusalem to Bethel, the religious capital of the Northern Kingdom. We are not sure just how long he preached in Bethel. We know that he delivered a powerful message to the throngs gathered for a religious festival. When he spoke against the surrounding nations the people were drawn to him to applaud his words with enthusiastic approval. They must have suffered severely under the blast of denunciation that followed.

Amaziah, the priest, was unable to stand up against the fierce preaching of the inspired prophet. He finally seized his only opportunity to interrupt and rebuke the intruder from the South. It was a classic encounter. The priest was bold because of the backing of the king; the prophet was bold from a sense of God's backing. Amaziah reported to the king immediately:

> *Amos hath conspired against thee in the midst of the house of Israel. The land is not able to endure all his words. For thus has Amos said, By the sword shall Jeroboam die.* (7:10b, 11a.)

It was a serious charge. George Adam Smith says: "Having fortified himself, as little men will do, by his duty to the powers that be, Amaziah dares to turn upon the prophet; and he does so, it is amusing to observe, with that tone of intellectual and moral superiority, which it is extraordinary to see some men derive from a merely official station or touch with government. . . . *Visionary, be gone! Get thee off to the land of Judah; and earn bread there, and there play the prophet. But at Bethel*—mark the rising accent of the voice—*thou shalt not again prophesy. The King's Sanctuary it is, and the House of the Kingdom.* With the official mind this is more conclusive than that it is the House of God! In fact the speech of Amaziah justifies the hardest terms which Amos uses of the religion of his day." [1]

The faithful prophet was, in the end, silenced by the hireling priest who sought to save himself and his position. Amos

[1] *The Book of the Twelve Prophets*, Vol. I, p. 114. Used by permission of the publishers, Harper & Brothers.

was driven away from Israel. Freedom of speech could not be allowed in Bethel. Neither an Elijah nor an Amos was ever safe in such a kingdom. This suppression and inhibition made it necessary for true prophets to retire to some quiet spot and think things through. Amos probably took up his lonely duties with the sheep and worked diligently to prepare his book for people who would be able to read and understand it.

His character. Amos was a simple, humble, plain man of God who was called from following a herd of sheep to hurl his messages into the ears of people who would have little respect for a man from the hills. He was blunt, direct, courageous and dynamic. He had a keen resentment against social wrongs. His righteous heart burned with anger when he saw the injustice and dishonesty of the cities. His sympathies were all with the poor. His peasant eyes flashed fire when he saw a palace. Luxury, extravagance and immorality were red flags in his face.

He was deeply religious. His keen insight into the deeper things of God was almost unbelievable. Possessing a world vision and a keen insight into the secrets of international politics he appeared to be a visionary among people whose heads were too thick to discern profound matters. His unflinching courage and his direct manner of presenting a blistering message against the rich, the influential and the powerful, mark him as a great crusader. He knew God, was certain of his call, felt the hand of God constantly upon him, and had no fear of any living person.

He was a man who had been molded by the stern discipline of the desert to look objectively upon persons, nations and events. The man in the Arabian desert lives alone. He is a nomad herdsman without any definite attachment to any government. Amos was certainly not a citizen of the Northern Kingdom. He could see Israel from the outside. He had but little sympathy for the king, the nobles, the army of the nation itself. This made him the more powerful in his denunciation of the citizens of that decaying nation.

An appraisal. Driver says of him: "He was no rustic in the ordinary sense of the word, he was a man of natural quickness and capacity, able to observe, to reflect, and to generalize, conscious of the breadth and scope of moral and spiritual realities, and impressive language." [2]

Cornill says: "Amos is one of the most wonderful appearances in the history of the human spirit." [3]

Cohon says: "Little hope to relieve the gloom, little faith in the God of mercy, who forgives and heals because of His infinite compassion, no trace of cheer, no inkling of a sense of humor—a grave fault which Amos shared with the rest of the prophets—no doubt in his own convictions mitigates the pronouncements of Amos. Hard, harsh, mercilessly dogmatic, he hurls denunciations at an unjust society and its flunkies. Uncompromising justice—that is the greatness and weakness of Amos." [4]

Eiselen says: "Amos was the first of the four eighth century prophets to redefine the Yahweh concept, and with him opened an era of constructive thinking hardly surpassed in any other period of human history." [5]

Storr says of him: "The desert, which has so often proved itself the cradle of religion, taught him by its sounds and silences to be spiritually alert, brought him face to face with God, fitted him to see human life in the light of the eternal moral verities, made him conscious of a vocation, and endowed him with the ethical austerity needed in one who was to be a prophet of judgment and denunciation. Sternness breathes in almost every line he wrote; he scornfully

---

[2] *Joel and Amos*, p. 105. Used by permission of the publishers, Cambridge University Press.

[3] *Prophets of Israel*, p. 42. Open Court Publishing Co., Chicago.

[4] *The Prophets*, p. 35. Used by permission of the publishers, Charles Scribner's Sons.

[5] *The Prophetic Books of the Old Testament*. (Vol. 2), p. 426. Used by permission of the publishers, Abingdon Press.

tears to shreds the popular sophistries of his day. He faces
up to the ultimate realities. For him God is a Living God,
a God of moral character, a God who acts in history, a God
who is a 'consuming fire.' " [6]

Harrell says: "The vastness and wonder of God's creation
gave him an uncommon breadth of vision. The spirit of
Amos was rugged like the rock-strewn hills of Tekoa, bold
like the winds of the desert, grand like the heavens that
stretched above him." [7]

Walker says: "If he had a tongue like a whip for the oppressor, it spoke out of a heart of love for the oppressed. He
was fierce because he was loving. His prophecy is molten
metal heated in the furnace of pity." [8]

James says: "How clearly he puts first things first. There
is a lift about this man, a freedom, a throwing off of ordinary
human hesitations that act as a tonic to our sluggish spirits.
Amos lives in a vaster world, where wealth and splendor
count for nothing, where kings seem small, where the power
of the powerful is contemptible and the only things worthy
of honour are justice and purity and truth, where what God
thinks is the supreme question. He is one of the great emanci-
pated spirits of the race. And he is one of its most passionate
champions of the poor. Whenever men have gone to the
Bible for encouragement in the long struggle for the libera-
tion of the underprivileged, they have found it chiefly in
Amos and in those successors whom he deeply influenced—
Isaiah and Micah." [9]

THE BOOK

When Amos found that the people would not hear him
in Israel he returned to Judah to put his messages in a book.
Much time and thought must have been given to produce

[6] *From Abraham to Christ*, p. 172. Hodder and Stoughton.
[7] *Ibid.*, p. 46.
[8] *Men Unafraid*, p. 32. Used by permission of the publishers, Abingdon
Press.
[9] *Ibid.*, p. 228.

this orderly arrangement of his sermons. The text has been carefully and faithfully preserved.

The psychological approach. Few instances in all literature surpass the keen approach that Amos makes to the assembled crowds at Bethel. It was a sacred feast day. A multitude of people had gathered to enter into the formal observance of a high day in Zion. They had no desire for a sermon that would cut them to the quick. This wise preacher from the wilderness was equal to the occasion. Beginning leisurely on Damascus he quickly caught their sympathetic attention. How they hated that wicked group at Damascus! Quickly he turned his withering broadside on Philistia, claiming to be a prophet from Yahweh with a genuine word against these bitter enemies of Israel. In rapid succession his sharp tongue lashed out upon Phoenicia, Edom, Ammon, Moab and then turned upon the land of Judah. What a wonderful preacher he was! The people must have been wild with frenzy as they followed with bated breath his every word. The finest psychologist of our day could not surpass this classic beginning. He was a master in his line. To be sure it was not merely a trick of the orator. These were genuine messages from God against sinning nations but we must give Amos credit for his admirable approach.

The style. It would be difficult to exaggerate in discussing the fine literary qualities of Amos' style. It has high literary merit. With very few exceptions the language is pure, the sentences are smoothly constructed, readable, clear, forceful and dramatic. The idiom is used beautifully to present his material with vividness and color. One gets the impression that a literary artist has been at work with all his tools and his colors to produce a masterpiece. He uses the metaphor, sarcasm, irony, parallelism, colorful imagery, eloquent phrases, effective contrasts, balanced clauses, and, in many instances, winged poetry of high quality. His diction is clear-cut and sinewy. One sees the orator at his best. His ardor and sincerity ring throughout all the speeches. There is passion and power in every line.

The outline. There are three well-defined parts.

1·2   Introduction. Judgments against the nations for their crimes.

    1:3-5 against Damascus for merciless cruelty in war.

    1:6-8 against Philistia for enslaving captives.

    1:9-10 against Tyre for dealing in slave traffic.

    1:11-12 against Edom for heartless, unbrotherly conduct.

    1:13-15 against Ammon for fiendish cruelty in war.

    2:1-3 against Moab for cruelty, hatred and inhuman treatment.

    2:4, 5 against Judah for disloyalty to Yahweh.

    2:6-16 against Israel for their outbroken sins against Yahweh.

3-6   Three messages against the crimes of Israel.

    3:1-15 The necessity for judgment on Israel.

    4:1-13 A denunciation of oppression, idolatry, and impenitence.

    5:1—6:14 Oppression, formal worship and vicious living spell the doom of Israel.

7-9   Five visions indicating God's determination to bring punishment on Israel.

    7:1-3 The locusts.

    7:4-6 The fire.

    7:7-9 A plumb-line.

    7:10-17 Historical narrative.

    8:1-3 A basket of summer fruit.

    9:1-10 The smitten sanctuary and its worshipers.

    9:11-15 An epilogue picturing the new day of power, splendor and peace.

The integrity of the book. Scholars are agreed that the book comes from the hand of Amos and that very few additions or changes have been made. It was probably composed during the months following his expulsion from Bethel. It shows the results of careful writing. The author started out with a very definite plan and carried it through to completion with directness and logical development. The majority of critics object to the genuineness of the prophecy against Judah in 2:4, 5 and the happy, hopeful picture in 9:8b-15. The "nature passages" in 4:13, 5:8, 9; 9:5, 6 are considered late. The arguments used in each case are far from conclusive.

The value of the book. This contemporaneous document of the most significant period of Old Testament prophecy is valuable for the Bible student. It is one of the earliest of the written prophetic messages and should prove exceptionally useful in getting a correct picture of these stirring days of the eighth century.

It pictures for us vividly and clearly the conditions of society in that half century. The careful student of the book can piece together the varied strands that make up a colorful picture of social conditions in Israel. Amos gives us the prejudices, the boastful optimism, the growth of power and wealth, the sense of security, the haughty attitudes, the increase of idleness and luxury, the corrupt government, the greedy women, the bribery, the immorality, the deep poverty and the suffering of the majority of the people.

He is just as clear in his vivid pictures of the religious conditions in Bethel. What a useless, insipid, inane type of religion! Amos, from his rare atmosphere in the desert, was strangely affected by the empty, formal, heartless thing that masqueraded under the name of religion. Instead of raising the standard of ethics and morality in the land it actually tended to degrade and lower the finer thoughts and sensibilities of the people. It was a positive disgrace. Amos pictures the people in a mad attempt to placate and please the national God with costly offerings, feasts, special days, gorgeous ritual and lavish outward signs of loyalty. Bethel, Beersheba, Dan and Gilgal were thronged with the trampling herd of deluded appeasers. Great slices of the newly found wealth

were poured out in these vain offerings. The keen prophet
of God saw with uncanny accuracy the heart behind this
stupid display. In stinging phrases he drew portraits of their
hearts as God saw them.

The book is especially valuable in the light it throws on
the available history and laws of God's Word. Amos seems to
be intimately acquainted with even the minute facts of history. Professor James Robertson says: "It is remarkable how
many allusions, more or less precise, to antecedent history
are found in the compass of this small book; and the significance of them lies not in the actual number of references,
but in the kind of references and the implications involved
in the individual references. That is to say, each reference is
not to be taken as an isolated testimony to some single event
in question, but involves a great deal more than is expressed,
and is intelligible only when other facts or incidents are
taken into consideration." [10] Amos took it for granted that
the people of the Bethel congregation knew the minute details of the patriarchal history such as we find in the Book
of Genesis. The Book of Amos gives us a valuable testimony
to the available literature of that day.

His messages are couched in language that breathes the
very spirit of the law given by Moses. The ethical demands
of the Book of the Law are the basis for the ethical challenges that he throws down to the people. One can hardly
escape the feeling that Amos was interpreting the *Torah* to
his hearers. It is a great experience to sit at the feet of such
an interpreter. He is a preacher of righteousness who is constantly throwing light on the Pentateuch.

From a study of this book we see an actual prophet at work
delivering his soul on subjects that God wanted presented
to His own people. We understand Yahweh and the Yahweh
religion better because of Amos. We see the prophets of the
schools in contrast to the true man of God. We understand
something of the requirements of a righteous God who claims

[10] International Standard Bible Encyclopedia, p. 123.

His chosen people and seeks to lift them into the rarer air by means of a faithful interpreter. The book helps us to see the early beginnings of the true prophetic order. It throws light on God's ideal prophet and the ideal religion.

PREACHING VALUES

In addition to the values we have noted it will be worth our while to look more definitely to the actual material for the building of sermons. The minister will want to know the Book of Amos.

His idea of God. It was given to this keen man from the desert to understand Yahweh better than any of his predecessors. He realized that Yahweh was not merely the private God of Israel. For Amos God is the great ruler of earth and sky, having created the massive mountains, the planets, the Pleiades, the seas, the wind, the clouds, and the people of the earth. Darkness flees away at His bidding; the waters rise and fall as He chooses; His angry breath dries up Carmel: locusts, mildew and plagues; pestilence, earthquakes and storms are brought upon the very spot He chooses. He is *Yahweh Sabaoth* with uncounted forces and powers in His hand to be used at any moment He selects.

He has the same right and control over the nations of the earth, moving them from one part of the earth to another, as a master chess player would move his pawns on the board. He can do as He wishes with Damascus, Gaza, Tyre, Edom, Moab and Ammon. Each of them will be judged at His judgment seat. Their gods, Hadad, Dagon, Melkart and Chemosh, are not even to be considered for a moment. In the past it was His hand that conducted the migrations of the Philistines from Caphtor and the Syrians from Kir. He is now ready to bring upon the nations one of His strongest powers.

Vividly he describes the impossibility of escape from the watchful eye of Yahweh. The maze of Carmel thickets, the lowest realms of Sheol, the highest heights of heaven, the trackless depths of the sea, and the far reaches of enemy territory would be useless as a hiding place. His glance penetrates equally into the spirit of men. It is an exalted conception of God that Amos teaches.

The Book of Amos makes it clear that Yahweh really cares for all nations with a genuine, intimate love. He has led other peoples as truly as He has led Israel. He will not favor Israel at the expense of the other nations. He wants to see all of His created ones blessed and following in His ways. He deals with each nation according to its own righteousness and punishes its sins impartially. Israel is to be judged by the same principles of common morality which are binding upon the surrounding tribes. Each must observe such basic rules of humanity as integrity, honesty, purity and the observance of worthy religious practices.

In no place does Amos deal with Yahweh's nature in an abstract manner. He pictures Him frankly as a moral being who knows Israel intimately, judges all peoples on moral grounds, and as a being who can be found only through moral conduct. It is utterly impossible to control or coerce Him but He is friendly and can be depended upon to do His part in promoting the happiness and success of men. Being an impartial judge His subjects may expect judgments on the basis of right and not colored by any previous appeasement or any sentimental consideration. Elaborate ritual only serves to offend His delicate sensibilities.

He is a God who will be forced to bring serious calamities and countless miseries on His people. Amos seems to think that Yahweh has reached the end of His patience with Israel. Retributive righteousness will bring the nations to the hour of ruin and disaster. Even the poor of the land who claim all of Amos' sympathies must go down along with their rich oppressors. Except for a few brief passages (notably 9:8-15) doom seems to be absolute. Many of our best scholars accept these verses as genuine words from the pen of Amos and thus give some light to a picture that is otherwise exceptionally dark. Amos knew God in such an intimate way that he found

great difficulty in getting across to selfish men the full beauty
of the divine character.

The Peril of Privilege. Amos had a very definite word to
say concerning the chosen people of God. In a real sense
Israel is a peculiar treasure of Yahweh. He has loved Israel
with a tender, compassionate love. She has been chosen as
His own treasured possession. While other peoples are in
His family it is upon Israel that He has directed His special
favors. This intimate relationship makes Israel's obligation
all the heavier. Privilege involves responsibility.

> *You only have I known of all the families of the
> earth: therefore I will visit upon you all your iniqui-*
> *ties* (3:2).

The goodness of God in electing Israel has increased her
responsibility. Amos teaches the true meaning of election.
To be "chosen ones of God" means heavier responsibilities,
and will bring upon them a punishment that is more severe.
Jesus taught the same truth:

> *To whomsoever much was given of him much will
> be required.* (Luke 12:48.)

George Adam Smith says: "Religion is no insurance against
judgment, no mere atonement and escape from consequences.
Escape! Religion is only opportunity—the greatest moral opportunity which men have, and which, if they violate, nothing remains for them but a certain fearful looking forward
unto judgment. You only have I known; and because you
did not take the moral advantage of my intercourse, because
you felt it only as privilege and pride, pardon for the past
and security for the future, therefore doom the more inexor-
able awaits you." [11]

Justice is elemental and eternal. God is righteous and He
must have honesty and fair dealings among His people. The
abuse of justice, the cruelty of the rich, the dishonest dealings

[11] *Ibid.,* p. 144.

of merchants and people, are not to be condoned by a righteous God. Amos attacks the sins of civilization. The inhumanities of the other nations are less cruel than the more refined sins of well dressed religious men and women who lived in Israel. Bribery, intolerance, luxury, oppression of the poor, and land-grabbing are more heinous in the eyes of Yahweh than all the atrocities of Semitic warfare. The social behavior of the people is more horrible than can be comprehended. He says:

> *They sell a righteous man for silver, and a needy man for a pair of shoes, who trample to the dust of the earth the head of the poor and pervert the way of the humble man . . . and on garments given in pledge they stretch themselves by every altar, and the wine of those who have been fined they drink in the house of their god. (2:6b-8.)*

Every phase of the social life is involved. The winter houses and the summer houses, the ivory houses and all other marks of godless extravagance will be swept away by the fierce breath of Yahweh. The cruel, heartless, brainless women come in for the bitterest denunciation that Amos delivers. Smith makes the following comment: "It is a cowherd's rough picture of women: a troop of kine—heavy, heedless animals, trampling in their anxiety for food upon every frail and lowly object in the way. But there is a prophet's insight into character. Not of Jezebels, or Messalinas, or Lady Macbeths is it spoken, but of the ordinary matrons of Samaria. Thoughtlessness and luxury are able to make brutes out of women of gentle nurture, with homes and a religion." [12] They were guilty of driving their husbands to fresh crimes in order to satisfy their selfish appetites and desires.

Amos laid the foundations deep and strong for the building Jesus was to erect. His austere sense of absolute righteous-

[12] *Ibid.*, p. 148.

ness made a standard that was far too high for the weak, flabby, stupid people of Israel. It was a worthy word in the midst of crime, selfishness, greed, oppression and dishonesty. Would that Amos might be heard today!

Thoughtless Unconcern. The prophet poured a volley of withering fire upon the people when he accused them of living in plenty, wasting valuable things, lolling about in extravagance while thousands suffered around them. They gave no thought to any poor creature who starved for want of food.

> *Woe unto them that are at ease in Zion and that trust in the mountain of Samaria, who designate themselves the first of the nations and unto whom the house of Israel cometh! Those who put far away the day of calamity and cause the seat of injustice to come near; who lie on ivory couches and sprawl on their divans, who eat the lambs from the flocks and calves from the midst of the stall, who twitter to the sound of the harp . . . who drink wine from bowls, and anoint themselves with the finest oils and grieve not for the affliction of Joseph.* (6:1-6.)

Israel is in a state of moral collapse. The stupid people do not care. The rich who have fine houses, tasty food, and plenty of wine are utterly indifferent to the cries, the groans, the poverty and the rights of poor people. Why should they worry about such insignificant matters? They can talk learnedly of art, commerce, business, patriotism, religion and politics, but not the slightest concern is felt or expressed concerning the real woes, the real dangers, the real sores of the people. Poverty, drunkenness, overwork, starvation, eviction from homes, and crimes are not to be considered in their busy lives. It has always been true that men and women who live well think of themselves as superior to the poor and to the less fortunate who are on the point of starving. It is a subtle temptation to set the mind on enjoying that which one has without thinking of the crying needs of unfortunate neighbors. Driver translates the last clause, *are not sick for the breach (or wound) of Joseph*. He says: "The words bring out the irony of their position: immersed themselves in a vortex of pleasure, they are unconcerned by the thought of the breach or wound in the body politic, i. e. the impending material ruin, the signs of which the prophet can only too clearly discern." [13] It is tragic that we find this same sin present in our own land. How thoughtless we are! How utterly unconcerned we find ourselves in the midst of approaching ruin! How unwilling we are to do something about the alleviation of suffering and distress!

Worship that insults God. Amos had a brand of religion that was truly spiritual. It had the essence of genuine heart-worship. The religion of the people of Israel was disgusting in his eyes. The people insulted God with their formal, heart-less, meaningless offering of sacrifices. He says:

> *I hate, I despise your feasts, and I take no delight in your festivals. Take away from me the noise of your songs; for I will not hear the melody of your harps. But let justice roll down as waters and right-eousness as an unfailing stream.* (5:21, 23, 24.)

He wants them to understand that they may not hope to win Yahweh's favor by a formal observance of rites and cere-monies. He does not ask for praise, sacrifices or ceremonial observances, but justice and righteousness. Conduct worthy of the presence of God is demanded. The most elaborate ceremony, observed in the most punctilious fashion, may not be used as a substitute for moral duties.

Amos did his best to help Israel see that the real heart of religion is ethical. They were allowing the ritual and the ceremonial to overpower the moral element. By the side of the smoking altar and the crowded church festivals there went up the cry of distress from the multitudes who were

[13] *Ibid.,* p. 199.

oppressed, the noise of wild revelry, the stench of dishonesty and bribery and the vilest sort of immorality. Their hearts and hands were unclean. God was insulted. Amos tried desperately to bring them to see the nature and essence of the religion of the Spirit.

Some practical lessons of permanent value. In addition to the five principal messages already given may we suggest some simple applications and inferences gleaned from the book.

1. Men displease God by hollow, insincere worship.
2. Nations and individuals that have been favored are laden with corresponding responsibilities.
3. God is gracious and patient in warning us.
4. Social injustice is intolerable to God.
5. Sin must be punished. Men must suffer.
6. Ease, luxury and idleness lead to open sin.
7. Possessing power over others creates grave dangers.
8. In any emergency God can raise up an effective prophet to do His will.
9. The discipline of the desert is valuable. What a great service the wilderness did to Amos!
10. God amply warns before He brings judgment, but He does not speak and warn endlessly.
11. Farley says: "Our solemn assemblies may still be despised by Yahweh. Whenever mere ritual and form are allowed to take the place of filial communion with God and moral obedience, our worship will be as lightly esteemed by Him as was the worship of Israel long ago, and our sanctuaries will fall, as did the ancient high places. Our churches will be empty, their services despised, and the heart and mind of men will turn for sustenance elsewhere." [14]

[14] *Ibid.*, p. 53.

ʼʼʼ HOSEA ʼʼʼ

IT IS STILL TRUE THAT "ALL THE WORLD LOVES A LOVER."
When we are confronted with the champion lover of all literature we may well pause to look with searching gaze upon him. Hosea takes his place among the greatest lovers of all the ages. His love was so strong that the vilest behavior could not dull it. He suffered severely but in each pang of suffering he came to know the infinite heart of God more clearly. Gomer broke his heart but she made it possible for him to give to the world a picture of the heart of the divine Lover. It will be a valuable study to analyze the character, the life, and the teachings of such a rare individual.

THE BACKGROUND

Historical and political. The reign of Jeroboam II in Israel was an era of peace, plenty, prosperity and luxury. In Samaria and in Jerusalem the people indulged in the kind of living that weakened and debauched them. They drifted thoughtlessly into ease, extravagance and oppression. The desert preacher, Amos, came to preach to them but his burning messages had little effect upon people who could not see any evidence of the serious consequences that the prophet predicted. As long as Assyria was quiet and the neighboring nations let them alone the Israelites were unwilling to think of any danger. Uzziah in Jerusalem and Jeroboam II in Samaria had their own way in the world. Two powerful kingdoms were built up that could hope to keep their place in the sun. Any secular commentator would be disposed to boast of the power and might and wealth of these two little nations. A true prophet of God was able to see signs of decay, evidences of poison in the blood stream, and inevitable calamity ahead for the stupid people.

Jeroboam's son, Zechariah, was murdered within six months after he had mounted the throne. His assassin, after a month as king, was dethroned and killed by the vigorous young Menahem. Anarchy was having its inning. No king was safe except as he was able to maintain a strong guard to keep assassins from him. Tiglath Pileser of Assyria began his spectacular career in 745 B.C. No kingdom was able to stand against his terrific onslaught. When he invaded the Westland Menahem was forced to pay an enormous tribute to satisfy the Assyrian demands. The Assyrian yoke was fastened securely upon the neck of Israel. Peace and safety and wealth were all taken away from the land.

Pekahiah was unable to carry on after the death of his father Menahem. Pekah took over the reigns of government and immediately set about to throw off the Assyrian yoke. Rezin of Damascus was glad to join him in this undertaking but Ahaz of Judah refused to take part in the conspiracy. It was a critical hour for all of them. When Pekah and Rezin made war on Judah the weak king Ahaz appealed to Tiglath Pileser for help. In a short while the great Assyrian army came to the rescue. Damascus was overthrown, Rezin was slain and practically all the kingdom of Israel was overrun. The city of Samaria was left with Hoshea, a puppet king, acting as ruler under the control of Assyria. Ahaz was forced to own Assyria as lord of Judah. Thus in just a few years the entire picture had completely changed. Amos had told them of the tragic consequences of their sins but they could not believe in the possibility of such calamities. When Hoshea proved faithless it became necessary for Shalmanezer to lay siege to the city of Samaria. After three years the end came for the stronghold founded by Omri.

It was during these years of anarchy, bloodshed, revolt and the break-up of a nation that Hosea the prophet preached in Israel. He was called upon to deliver God's message to a people who had very little concern for spiritual matters. They had not listened to Amos. They were not disposed to give heed to Hosea. Dissolution, decay and death were all around him. Anarchy, chaos, feuds and broken covenants were visible on every side. Wild adventurers could arise to murder a king and seize the throne at almost any stage of the journey. These foolish and godless rulers sought to further their own selfish schemes while the nations suffered and crumbled. External enemies and internal feuds brought about the downfall of the two hundred year old kingdom of Jeroboam I. Silly princes who led the people to trust in Egypt hastened the end. Egypt promised much but was never able to carry out any of her promises. She was utterly useless as an ally.

In the South, Jotham and Ahaz reigned as kings while Isaiah and Micah brought God's messages as prophets. Hosea stood his ground in the North as God's representative in those troublous days.

Social conditions. On every side the young prophet faced social conditions that made his heart sick. The general feeling on every side made for laxness and looseness in personal behavior. The rulers set poor examples for the people. Property had little value, for no person could be sure of his right to keep it. The courts were corrupt. Judges made their living from bribes and excessive fees wrung from helpless people who sought to hold on to their property and their rights. Conspiracies and plots were so common that the people did not dare trust any group. Amos had watched the ease-loving people loll in idleness and luxury. Hosea saw those same people hardened and made criminal by the conditions that surrounded them. Literal bloodshed, highway robbery, murder and organized vice were visible on every hand. The priests who were God's chosen representatives were actually at the head of organized bandit gangs. They were the instigators of rackets. In an unstable world the people had come to lose their self-reliance. Fear and uncertainty gripped them to render them helpless.

Family life had gone to pieces. Regard for the sanctity of

the home and the marriage vow had been lost. The false worship and foreign cults had broken down the old standards of morality and faithfulness. It is a tragic hour when men and women lose the sense of the sacredness of home relationships. Drunkenness with all of its attendant evils was fast breaking down the home life and debauching the minds of the people.

The concentration of wealth in the hands of a few had borne its natural fruits in class hatreds, in oppressive measures, in eviction from homes, in desperate deeds of retaliation, and in actual slavery for many of those who could not cope with their environment. So much abject poverty in the midst of arrogant men and women with wealth must have caused a trying situation for a prophet who sensed something of God's hatred for such conditions.

Religious conditions. In addition to social conditions that were the outgrowth of sin, we must look for a few moments on the actual state of the hearts that produced such ugly fruit. Sin ruled in all their hearts. The priests had failed in their high duty of leading the people to know God's Word and His requirements for them. These priests had actually led the people into sin and had made sinning attractive. Moral and ethical requirements were eliminated. The sort of worship arranged for the worshipers was formal and professional. When priest and ritual made no high demands on the people it became increasingly difficult to keep the human hearts from sinning. It became the fashion of the day to live lives that lacked moral tone and then go on in the worship at the sanctuary in reckless abandon. The licentious rites, taken over from rank paganism, led the worshipers to such excesses that all thought of purity and spiritual living was out of the question. The so-called "holy women" were kept at the central sanctuaries as temple prostitutes to gratify the lusts of the men. The people rapidly became degenerate. Family life was rotten. Husbands would go out in sinful debauchery only to find their wives and daughters as guilty as they were. Hosea looked upon an unspeakable tragedy in Yahweh's land.

The idol worship and the worship of the gods of the surrounding nations caused the very heart of God to weep in sorrow. Hosea sensed something of the heinousness of the sin of unfaithfulness that caused Yahweh so much heart sorrow. He represents Israel as saying:

> *Let me follow my paramours who are giving me*
> *my bread and my water, my wool and my flax, my*
> *oil and my drink.* (2:5)

She is interested in any god who will furnish for her the material things she craves. Being ignorant of the true Giver she will grope in indecision in search of the best among substitutes.

Even in this "delirious dance of death" the people are brazen in their ungodly self-conceit. They are quoted as saying:

> *I have indeed grown rich,*
> *I have found wealth for myself.* (12:8)

The mercenary nation refuses to see the stark tragedy of the picture that spreads out on every side. It is much easier to imagine that all is well and that no harm can possibly come to one who has been so wise as to fortify himself with wealth and provisions and all available protections. This mad delusion of self-conceit when they were seated on a raging volcano must have made the heart of Hosea weep with strange grief.

It must be remembered that Hosea was preaching to people who had been God's chosen ones for many generations. They had failed to understand and follow the teachings of the law and the prophets. They were guilty of a heinous sin in that they had refused to love One who had loved them so devoutly. They had answered true love with infidelity. A covenant had been broken. A God who had chosen them, brought them out of Egypt, loved them through terrible trials, and established them in the promised land, had been deserted and spurned. Surely it was a heart-rending experience. The prophet whose heart had been broken was chosen to speak to this sinning people.

George L. Robinson has suggested the following successive steps in Israel's national downfall:

1. Lack of knowledge. 4:6, 11. *My people are destroyed for lack of knowledge.*

2. Pride. 5:5. *And the pride of Israel doth testify to his face.*

3. Instability. 6:4. *For your goodness is as a morning cloud, or as the dew that goeth early away.*

4. Worldliness. 7:8. *Ephraim mixeth himself with the peoples; Ephraim is a cake unturned.*

5. Corruption. 9:9. *They have deeply corrupted themselves as in the days of Gibeah.*

6. Backsliding. 11:7. *My people are bent on backsliding from me.*

7. Idolatry. 13:2. *And now they sin more and more and have made themselves molten images of their silver, even idols, according to their own understanding.*[1]

The Man of God

Hosea was a native son who loved his own land and his people so devotedly that he constantly referred to them in pictures that cannot be forgotten. He came to his own people and spent his entire life in an unceasing effort to call them back to God. No other nations claimed his attention except as they were vitally connected with the welfare of Israel.

His marriage. Early in his life he fell in love with and married Gomer the daughter of Diblaim. He probably knew very little about her history or her character. Love has a way of causing one to forget such considerations. We do know

---

[1] *The Twelve Minor Prophets,* p. 23. Harper & Brothers.

that he loved her devotedly and that he was willing to take an oath of allegiance that was to continue all through his life. We learn of her own shallow, senseless sort of thought of him that was to cause such agony and suffering. She had no way of understanding the mighty love of Hosea. She proved herself unworthy of such love but the lover kept on loving her. We can never know the poignant suffering of those hours when his heart yearned for the sweetheart of his youth. Her silly, thoughtless behavior only added to the tragedy.

At least three interpretations of the account of his marriage have been advanced. (1) Some commentators claim that the account is literal history and that Hosea was commanded to marry an actual adulteress and that he obeyed the divine command. (2) Many have considered it an allegory, claiming that no such marriage took place but that the preacher invented the parable to illustrate the conception of the love of God for sinful men. (3) The majority of the interpreters hold to the view that Hosea actually married Gomer who was at the time of the marriage a clean woman but that she later fell into sin.

Each of these interpretations has had a strong group of advocates. In the light of the whole message of the book it seems inconceivable that either the first or the second can be true. The idea that Hosea is illustrating is that Israel was pure and innocent and faithful when Yahweh chose her as His bride. Hosea had such high ideals of marriage and preached such strong messages against infidelity that we cannot imagine his going out to a woman of impure life and taking her into his own home. Surely he married a woman who was pure and worthy. She became entangled in the web of sin and immoral life about her and became an adulteress after the birth of the first child. The intense pain that came to the pure heart of the husband cannot be weighed. The struggle of his grief and shame when he found that she was unfaithful to him reveals something of the inexhaustible love of the true lover. After several years of the agony she went out from the home to sell herself into slavery to the paramours who promised her more. What a tragic picture of the downward road of those who trample the pure love of God under foot to go in pursuit of the lovers who promise illegitimate pleasures. Yahweh of Hosts suffers excruciating agony of heart when His own loved ones prove false just as the sensitive young husband suffered when he realized that his dearest possession had sold herself to others and left him alone.

His equipment. The young prophet received from God a special endowment of soul that fitted him to sense and catch the keener things of the divine revelation. His sensitive soul gave him a decided advantage over other interpreters of the deeper mysteries of grace. He was profoundly influenced by Amos who had such a difficult time in getting men to know Yahweh as he knew Him. In a land as small as Israel it is out of the question to suppose that the young preacher failed to hear and appreciate and profit by the spiritual challenges laid down by the older prophet from Tekoa. Hosea seems to have had a distressingly tender place in his heart for his land and his own people. His love for his neighbors fitted him to preach with peculiar effectiveness to them. He knew their sins, their lives, their failures, their responsibilities. His knowledge of nature and his intimate acquaintance with every phase of the nation's life prepared him to call them back to his beloved Yahweh.

The black domestic tragedy did something for him that nothing else could have done. Not until a heart is crushed by love's indescribable sorrow is it truly fitted to preach the deeper things of God's matchless love. The shattered romance of his life led him to see another romance. He saw the picture of Yahweh wooing and marrying a poor slave girl in the land of Egypt. Watching Him lavish His tender love on her and the infidelity with which she treated His tenderness, Hosea was able to see God's inexhaustible love as no other prophet had understood it. He grew into a prophet who had power in presenting the deeper qualities of God's most glorious attributes.

His character. Hosea was a quiet, pensive, affectionate, sensitive young man who surrendered his heart to preach when he became so painfully conscious of the suffering love of a Father God. He was more than a realist with a captivating style. He was keen to perceive the hidden depths of religion and life. He learned to know Yahweh so well that he was in possession of an understanding of God hitherto unknown. He was intensely sensitive. Walker says of him: "Like a radiophone he caught the music of the spheres, but like the delicate seismograph that registers an earthquake in any part of the earth's surface, his sensitive soul recorded the hidden and secret rumblings of divine judgment. This sensitiveness made him at the same time one of the gladdest and one of the saddest of men. He had drunk as deeply of the springs of joy as of the cup of woe." [2]

Hosea lived such a lonely life that his whole ministry was tinged with a strange note of sadness. His people hurt him almost as deeply as his prodigal wife had wounded him. In spite of this distress of soul he was a confirmed optimist. He saw something of the tremendous love of God for sinful men and sensed the victory that such love would ultimately win. He believed that God, with all His resources of loving ingenuity, would at length prevail for the salvation of His chosen people. The prophet of the broken heart was made to lean heavily on his Father God and thus to discover the promise of victory.

An appraisal. It will be of special interest to Bible students to note some of the estimates of Hosea given by scholars.

Cadman says: "No prophet of Israel outranked him in appreciation of the Eternal mercy. The perfect love which casts out fear involves mutual choice, mutual confidence, mutual trust. In these ways Hosea interpreted the unique message dictated by his afflicted heart. Through purgatorial means he

[2] *Ibid.,* p. 51.

obtained his knowledge of the God who suffers because He loves His chosen ones, and who will not cease to love them while hope remains that they may yet love Him." [3]

Ward says: "It was Hosea's privilege to interpret the Eternal in the selfless endeavor of forgiving love." [4]

Robinson says: "One general lesson is taught by Hosea of ever permanent worth, namely, that inward corruption in a nation is more dangerous to its existence than their external enemies. And a kindred lesson closely related to this is: that the truest of all patriots is he who, like Hosea, identifies himself with his people, sorrows over their calamities as though they were his own, and repents for their sins as though he had committed them himself." [5]

Kirkpatrick says: "He gains in depth what he loses in breadth. If the teaching of Amos is wider, that of Hosea is more profound. . . . Hosea goes deeper, and deals not with action only but with the springs and motives of action." [6]

Cohon says: "Hosea presents a striking contrast to Amos and, in the end, supplants him. Amos thunders the stern, unbending justice and wrath of God. Hosea pleads, exhorts, and woos in the name of the loving-kindness of God. Amos is concerned with man's disloyalty to God." [7]

Walker says: "This sensitiveness accounts for another peculiarity of Hosea: his curious combination of tenderness and fierceness. His sense of the love of God made him very tender, and his sense of the way in which this love was outraged made him like a lion fierce for prey. The lightning flashed from his tear-dimmed eyes. He flames like a volcano, and then appears like a delicate and fragrant lily." [8]

Storr says: "Hosea, disciplined by the agony of a private

[3] *Ibid.*, p. 44.
[4] *Ibid.*, p. 92.
[5] *Ibid.*, p. 26.
[6] *The Doctrine of the Prophets*, p. 138. Used by permission of the publishers, The Macmillan Company.
[7] *Ibid.*, p. 49.
[8] *Ibid.*, p. 52.

grief, wounded where his love was tenderest, learned that there was sorrow in the divine heart; passed behind God as Law to God as Love; did not forget judgment, but felt that he had more chance to win his people to repentance if he put pleading before threatening, and set forth the pain of God rather than the anger of God." [9]

James says: "Undoubtedly it is in his teaching of the love of God that Christians of today discover Hosea's chief value. It had two corollaries. One was that suffering for sin, though necessary, is educational; the other, that God never gives up but will have His loving way at last." [10]

Merrill says: "We bless the God of the prophets for this true and beautiful spirit that, out of an experience that would have left most of us crushed and embittered and hopeless, won his way to light and truth, and left for us men and for our salvation the clear, undying truth that God is love, and wants from us, above all, love like His own. In coming near to Hosea, we come very near to Christ." [11]

Bewer says: "Hosea deepened and intensified religion, but he also narrowed it in this exclusive possession of one by the other. The spiritualization and refinement of religion is his great contribution. His joining of love with righteousness also in the relation of man to man meant much for social ethics, for the healing of society is possible only by righteousness and love." [12]

Harper says: "If Amos' message was universal, Hosea's was more narrowly national; if Amos' was ethical, Hosea's was religious. There is no lack of the tender and the spiritual element. While Amos was broader, Hosea goes deeper; Amos is controlled solely by the ethical spirit, Hosea by the religious spirit." [13]

[9] *Ibid.,* p. 184.
[10] *Ibid.,* p. 245.
[11] *Prophets of the Dawn,* p. 91. Used by permission of the publishers, Fleming H. Revell Co.
[12] *The Literature of the Old Testament,* p. 98.
[13] I.C.C., *Amos and Hosea,* p. cliv, cxlviii.

Harrell says of Hosea: "For pathos and beauty his book is unsurpassed in the Old Testament. He felt the moral decay of his people as keenly as Amos, but above the confusion of his time his voice is heard, like a plaintive song in the midst of the storm: *O Israel, return unto Jehovah thy God.* Amos was a preacher to the conscience; Hosea was a preacher of repentance." [14]

THE BOOK

The casual reader will find difficulty in finding the plan or the outline of Hosea's book. The author did not arrange his paragraphs in logical order or develop his arguments logically. He was so deeply stirred by a great emotion that he jumped from one great idea to another with very little regard for order. Davidson said in his defense, that the book is but little more than "a succession of sobs." Some one else has compared it to the diary of a soldier at the front written between the explosion of shells. Cheyne says: "Even the fetters of grammar are almost too much for Hosea's vehement feelings." [15] Even though it is so disconnected one does not have much difficulty in understanding the great, throbbing purpose of his soul. Perhaps no book we read will come nearer leaving us with a clear understanding of the burden that rests upon the soul of the author. He is desperately in love and keeps on sobbing his heart out while he repeats his love story. It may reasonably well be compared to a great ocean liner that seems to toss aimlessly in a heavy sea, yet a careful examination assures the mind that she is plowing her way with strong power on her charted course. The whole prophecy is an unceasing cry of anguish as he comes over and over to a heedless nation with his call to repent and come back to the God who loves them with an undying love. He pictures God as desperately crushed with strong emotion as He looks upon people who have spurned His love and

[14] *Ibid.,* p. 59.
[15] *Hosea,* p. 33. Used by permission of the publishers, Cambridge University Press.

turned their back on the marriage vow. It is a tender appeal of a true lover whose heart is broken within him.

Professor Harper says: "There is manifestation everywhere of contending and conflicting feelings; of tenderness side by side with indignation, of love and hate commingled; of leniency passing swiftly into severity and the reverse, and of hope for the future actually turning before the gaze into an almost absolute despair. . . . But Hosea is not illogical as he has so frequently been represented. His ability to give expression to a system of theology which was to serve henceforth as the basis of all Israelitish thought, is a factor worthy of consideration in any estimate of his character." [16]

The outline. In general we may divide the book into two sections: chapters 1-3 give us a record of Hosea's own tragic experiences and their message to his heart. Chapters 4-14 preserve for us the message Hosea delivered to his people. In them he sets forth the causes of Israel's downfall—lack of knowledge, pride, instability, sinful alliances, a godless monarchy, a corrupt religion and continual backsliding. He closes with three chapters offering complete forgiveness to repenting sinners.

Brice gives the following outline: [17]

1:2-3:5	The sin against *trust.*
4:1-6:11	The sin against *truth.*
7:1-13:16	The sin against *troth.*
14:1-9	The final appeal

G. Campbell Morgan summarizes it as follows:

"We find in it first a clear revelation of God's attitude towards sin, distinct affirmations concerning His activity in judgment upon sin, and supremely a declaration of the appeal of His love. Three words, then, indicate the lines, namely, sin, judgment, love. These three things merge into the perfect music of the prophecy." [18]

[16] *Ibid.,* p. CXIV.
[17] *Seers of Israel,* p. 25-27. Marshall, Morgan and Scott.
[18] *Voices of Twelve Hebrew Prophets,* p. 44. Fleming H. Revell.

Integrity. In former times the entire book was accepted as coming from the pen of Hosea. Modern criticism has attacked the integrity of the book and made it the work of later editors who have changed it at will to say what they want said. They find some passages in the midst of the chapters dealing with Judah. Since Hosea preached in Israel it is not considered proper for him to include the Southern Kingdom in his prophecies. Another matter of more serious moment is the proposal to eliminate the sections that have a hint of divine forgiveness in them. Since Hosea is a prophet of doom it seems hardly probable that he would include such hopeful passages as the book contains. Professor Crafer says: "In support of the integrity of the book and the gospel of hope as preached by Hosea, it may be urged, among many other considerations, (1) that it would be monstrous for the prophet to have hope for his own erring wife to the end, and yet declare that God had finally flung off faithless Israel, whether they repented or not; (2) that chapter XIV shews no change in style, and is one of the most exquisite passages in the book, and yet its tender promise would have to be ascribed to some later editor or interpolator." [19]

SOME PREACHING VALUES

Great Religious Ideas: Hosea made a vital contribution to the thinking of his people and the thought life of succeeding generations.

1. THE KNOWLEDGE OF YAHWEH. The young preacher's heart was torn and crushed because Gomer did not understand him. She was utterly incapable of such knowledge. The years of intimate association with this keen, tender, mystical, spiritual giant should have made her conscious of the tremendous worth of the man. She never knew him. His heart must have been deeply hurt as he realized how shallow she was in such a vital matter.

He represents Yahweh as a Sufferer who has found His

[19] *The Book of Hosea,* p. 19. Cambridge University Press.

love unrequited. The people do not know their God. They are stupid, without intelligence, insensible to all that is high and holy, and above all they are not even conscious of the love of God for them. Their teachers—the priest and prophets—are largely to blame for this lack of understanding. Since they are unaware of the true nature of God's purpose for them they cannot understand the loyalty, the love, the service that should characterize one who is in covenant relation with a gracious God.

God has been active in His efforts to reveal Himself and His will to men. Through the years God has used prophets, great deliverances and gracious kindnesses to lead them to know Him. Real love should have the power of eliciting love in return. Patiently, solicitously, graciously He has given Himself to them. His heart breaks when He realizes that they are woefully weak in their consciousness of the ever-present Character who hovers about them. If they could only come to know Him! Hosea pictures Yahweh as a great Lover who is willing to go to any lengths to cause His people to pause, look upon, and come to know the great Lover who is wooing them. How earnestly He tries to attract them to Himself!

2. THE PICTURE AND NATURE OF SIN. Hosea looked through the lexicon for the ugliest word that he could find and used it to represent sin. To him sin is essentially unfaithfulness. When one ceases to love God and turns himself to follow some other being he is guilty of the tragic sin. What God wants is a genuine love from hearts that cannot even think of loyalty to another being.

Sin ages one and destroys his youthful spirit. The decay is gradual, imperceptible, but dangerous and fatal. Working secretly and silently it accomplishes the ruin of the stupid individual (5:12; 7:9).

Sin is contagious and one who exposes himself to the atmosphere and presence of those whose influence is bad cannot hope to escape its certain consequences (4:9). The foul sins practiced at the sanctuaries have their influence in the homes of the people. The men return from wild orgies only to find their wives and daughters guilty of the same low sins (4:14). The nation becomes sterile and God's purpose for its future is thwarted.

Sin's effects are as certain and as natural as the power of gravity (8:7). Each succeeding zephyr blown into the air returns as a boomerang in a devastating whirlwind. Sin can end only in captivity, for the heart is rotten to the center and calamity must come to burn out the serious infection in the blood stream of the nation.

Sin robs a people of the power to make moral distinctions (4:11). Moral appreciation is impossible when the optic nerve of the soul has been impaired. Nothing can restore the diseased muscles that control the finer decisions of the mind.

3. GENUINE REPENTANCE: Hosea insists that each man needs to turn about and come home to God (3:5; 5:4; 6:1; 14:1, 2). In a real sense the nation is considered an individual. God's covenant with them is as sacred and binding as a marriage vow. The prophet has in mind a tender call to his wife to cease following the new lovers and return to her lawful husband. It is this same plea that he pictures God as making to the sinful nation. Israel is His own bride. He loves her, wants her, is waiting lovingly for her return, will welcome her with outstretched arms and forgive her freely.

George Adam Smith says: "To Hosea repentance is no mere change in the direction of one's life. It is a turning back upon one's self, a retracing of one's footsteps, a confession and acknowledgment of what one has abandoned. The return to God like the New Testament *Metanoia,* is the effect of new knowledge; but the new knowledge is not of new facts—it is of facts which have been present for a long time and which ought to have been appreciated before. Of these facts Hosea describes three kinds: the nation's misery, the unspeakable grace of their God, and their great guilt in turning from Him. Again it is as in the case of the prodigal: his hunger, his father, and his cry, 'I have sinned against

Heaven and in thy sight.' Repentance is no mere turning or even re-turning. It is a deep and an ethical process—the breaking up of fallow ground, the labour and long expectation of the sower, the seeking and waiting for Jehovah till Himself send the rain." [20]

4. THE LOVE OF GOD: Hosea's sense of the infinite love of God made it possible for him to understand the true nature of human sin. It thrills the prophet to catch a glimpse of the tender love of God manifesting itself all the way down through the years (11:1, 3). The bonds of love have been drawing the weak, adopted children along through the wilderness journey. A father's love has been in evidence each step of the way. That love has survived all the cruel slights, the unfaithfulness, the disloyalty, and the callous indifference of the years. God is limited in His power to command it. The sinners may reject Him and refuse to return His gracious love. He may woo them and heap gifts upon them but He may yet fail in His purpose of winning them. He has so limited Himself that He is helpless before a stubborn or insensible sinner. His love can be resisted. In the great divine heart there is an unending conflict between His hatred of sin and His love of the sinner. In Him there is unspeakable tenderness toward the sinner and unspeakable indignation over sin and ingratitude.

5. THE WAY OF SALVATION: Hosea pictures God as one who is so deeply in love that He will not be turned aside in His search for His people. His love shall not fail. He will not let go until love has had its way and victory crowns His efforts. Hosea knew God well enough to understand that it would be possible to follow on through the years until the exile would burn out the sin and teach the people the pure essence of religion. They would then hear the divine call to their hearts.

Just as Hosea went to the market place to buy back his wayward wife and bring her to his home again so would the

[20] *Ibid.*, p. 345.

great Lover redeem and bring back His own bride. The prophet sees a vision of God waiting, yearning, pursuing, wooing, winning, redeeming and restoring His wandering wife. Surely God can make the way of salvation possible.

SOME GREAT TEXTS

She said:

> *I will go after my paramours, who give my bread and my water, my wool and my flax, my oil and my drink. And she did not notice that it was I who gave her the wheat, and the wine, and the oil, and multiplied to her the silver and the gold which they used for Baal.* (2:5, 8.)

These verses give us a tragic picture of an ignorant, senseless, misguided wife who blindly resolves to follow the lure of lovers who promise to satisfy her low appetites. Israel had remained outwardly loyal to Yahweh but had sought to bring some magic touch to her fields, her orchards, her flocks and her herds by looking to the local Baals. She was willing to sell herself for mere material rewards.

God wants her to understand that these Canaanite lovers are utterly helpless to give her the gifts for which she follows them. God has control of the corn, the flax, the wool and all such material things. He is deeply grieved that she is unconscious of the fact that these had been gifts from the hand of God. God's lavish treasures have been poured out upon the altars of her shame.

> *Therefore, behold, I will woo her, and cause her to get into the wilderness and I will speak to her heart. And I will betroth thee to me in faithfulness and thou wilt know Yahweh.* (2:14, 19, 20.)

What a beautiful picture of the inextinguishable love of the Lord seeking His own willful bride! What purposes of grace He has in store for the one He wooed and won in the

desert journey! What memories of the old honeymoon days!
The happy days of the first betrothal are to be renewed. He
believes that He will be able to win her to Himself again.
She will *sing* again as in the "good old days." He promises
that the ugly past will be forgotten and that the new marriage will be an eternal affair. Grace will bear its fruit. The
new betrothal is to be in *righteousness,* in *judgment,* in
loving-kindness, in *faithfulness.* The picture of *speaking to
the heart* is one of the tenderest figures in all literature.

> *So I bought her to me for fifteen pieces of silver,
> and a homer and a half of barley.* (3:2.)

His love is constant in spite of adultery, lack of love,
broken vows and desertion. He was happy to redeem her,
purify her, and take her back into his home and his heart.
She had descended to a wretched and degraded place as a
slave-concubine to her lovers. The price he paid was the
price demanded for a common slave. The fifteen shekels
was one half the price designated in Exodus 21:32. The
measure and a half of barley probably made up for the other
half. Following the public buying of his wife he was to leave
her for a number of months in seclusion until she could be
declared fit to come into his home again. Hosea learned that
God was ready and willing and anxious to seek, forgive, redeem and purify Israel (cf. Isa. 52:3; 44:22).

G. A. Smith says: "The story of the wife's unfaithfulness
had come before that of Israel's apostasy. It was not he who
set God, but God who set him, the example of forgiveness.
The man learned God's sorrow out of his own sorrow; but
conversely he was taught to forgive and redeem his wife
only by seeing God forgive and redeem the people." [21]

> *Because there is no truth, or love, or knowledge of
> God in the land. Swearing and lying, and killing,
> and stealing, and committing adultery, they break*

[21] *Ibid.,* p. 250.

out, blood touches blood. My people perish for lack
of knowledge. (4:1, 2, 6.)

How unspeakably tragic! What a picture of the actual social and religious situation! The utter corruption of the nation is traced to irreligion. They do not know Yahweh.
Imagine the patriot listing the assets and liabilities of his
native land. The three desirable qualities without which a
nation is bankrupt are entirely lacking. Fidelity, brotherly
love, and a knowledge of Yahweh cannot be found anywhere.
The careful diagnosis reveals an abundance of those things
that make a true patriot blush with shame. Swearing, lying,
murder, theft, and adultery fill the land. The covenant rati-
fied at Sinai has been broken. The ninth, sixth, eighth, and
seventh commandments have been most completely broken.
Lack of knowledge of God always leads to moral corruption
and anarchy.

> *For my people are like their priest. My people per-*
> *ish for lack of knowledge. They feed on the sin of*
> *my people and set their heart on their iniquity. And*
> *it has come to be like people, like priest: and I will*
> *punish them for their ways—because they have left*
> *off heeding Yahweh. (4:4, 6, 8, 9.)*

The spiritual guides are the real offenders. The tragic situation is due to the faithless, profligate priests who have led
the people into ignorance and sin. The teachers are the
leaders in vice and corruption. Fines and sin-offerings and
fees enrich the ones who should be giving their lives to teach
truth, reverence, honesty and the *Torah* of God. These
priests are rejected by a holy God who despises both their
teaching and their conduct. Their regard for the true essence
of religion has rendered them worse than useless in the life
of the people. Ignoring the high privilege of their sacred
office they have reduced themselves to the spiritual level of
the ones who should be lifted by them.

Machiavelli said: "We Italians are more irreligious and corrupt than others—because the Church and her representatives set us the worst example." [22]

> *Whoredom and wine and new wine take away the understanding. For a spirit of harlotry has led them astray, and they have played the harlot away from their God—*
> *Yea, a people stupid and falling to ruin.* (4:11, 12, 14.)

Sin takes its tragic toll. Hosea bluntly states the effect of absorption in ritual, indulgence of the lusts of the body and the immoral worship at the sanctuaries. He claims that "sin cuts the optic nerve of the soul" and renders it incapable of making moral distinctions. What a keen observation! Spiritual perception is impossible. The brain is clouded. The mind is weakened. The people are utterly stupid. The power of moral appreciation is gone completely. What a lesson for the people of any age! There was a time in their lives when they could make moral distinctions. Sin has brought about the inevitable destruction of the powers of perception. When that has happened the religious ideals and practices are lowered until the whole community suffers.

> *Ephraim is wedded to idols; let her alone.* (4:17. cf. 5:4.)

Since the pollution is so deep the prophet gives utterance to his most solemn statement. Yahweh has already exhausted every possible means for their recovery. The only remedy left is to abandon Israel to the school of bitter experience. Ephraim is wedded (mated) to her idols. She is stubborn and willful. She must learn in the cruel crucible of experience that she has fallen far from God. How serious is the offense! God's purpose for Israel includes a full restoration to favor

[22] Quoted by Gore in *The New Commentary on the Holy Scriptures,* p. 559.

and full participation in the joys of the restored community but not until the suffering and purging of the exile has been accomplished. His method involved leaving her to face spiritual desolation and famine until she turned back to her God.

> *Come, and let us return to Yahweh: For he has torn, that he may heal us. And let us know, let us follow on to know Yahweh; whenever we seek him we shall find him.* (6:1, 3.)

These words are the cry of a repentant, returning remnant which has learned to know Yahweh in the furnace of suffering. She recognizes that her punishment has been richly deserved and that it has come directly from God. She determines to go for healing to him who has been waiting so patiently for her return.

The sequel shows that these beautiful words represent an external repentance only—a fitful turning to God on the part of people who have never understood the serious nature of their offense and are still utterly ignorant of the true nature of the God whom they have so foolishly provoked. They are thinking of an easily satisfied deity who has no moral or ethical standard of righteousness. It hurts to see God's chosen people in such dense ignorance concerning the deeper things of revealed religion.

> *What can I do with thee, Ephraim? What can I do with thee, Judah? Since your love is like a morning cloud, and like the dew which goes early away Therefore have I hewn them by the prophets; and my judgment is like the light that goes forth. But it is love that I have desired and not sacrifice: and the knowledge of God rather than burnt offerings.* (6:4-6. cf. Matt. 9:13; 12:7.)

Here we have the heart cry of a noble lover who has been crushed by the ingratitude and broken vows of the one he has loved. The penitence expressed in verses 1-3 is only "skin-

deep." The great Lover is now in despair over the fickleness
of Ephraim and Judah. The tender feelings of the early
honeymoon days have vanished as the dew before the sun.
Their poor shallow hearts are incapable of true love. Sin
has rendered them callous and unresponsive. Prophets have
slashed and cut with withering words but still the heart does
not know genuine love.

They still labor under the impression that forgiveness can
be won by bringing the prescribed sacrifices at stated inter-
vals. Such behavior, even though it may qualify as to correct-
ness of detail in forms and ceremonies, is hollow mockery.
God wants righteous conduct, "leal" love, devoted loyalty of
heart more than sacrifices and outward conformity to ritual
requirements.

Amos, Isaiah and Jeremiah do their best to drive this
thought home to people who have no basis for a clear understanding of such vital matters. Jesus quotes this verse twice in
His teaching ministry. (Matt. 9:13 and 12:7.) (cf. also Amos
5:21-24; I Sam. 15:22; Isa. 1:11ff; Mic. 6:6f; Jer. 7:22f; and
Ps. 51.)

> *Ephraim mixes himself among the nations; Ephraim
> has become a cake not turned. Strangers have de-
> voured his strength but he knows it not: yea, gray
> hairs are sprinkled upon him, but he knows it not.
> They do not return to Yahweh their God, nor seek
> him, for all this. And Ephraim has become like
> a silly dove, without understanding: they cry to
> Egypt, they go to Assyria. (7:8-11.)*

How terrific are the consequences of wickedness! Hosea has
been dealing with the moral element in the life of Israel. He
now turns to a discussion of the political decay which is a
sign of her moral decay. It is a keen analysis that he gives us
of the effects of impurity upon both the intellectual vigor
and the reproductive powers of the nation.

Israel has been called to separate herself from the peoples

of Palestine and "dare to be different." Hosea finds that she has been confronted with lavish commerce, alien tempers and fashions, foreign gods and low ideals, but does not possess the moral fibre needed to withstand such strong currents. Being weak and ignorant of God she has been utterly defeated and has been impressed by foreign people instead of making a definite impression *upon* them.

These two epigrams reveal the weakness of the foreign and the domestic policies of Israel. She has dissipated her natural strength and character by mixing with her neighbors. It is a serious moment when one is led to dissipate moral energy by compromise, by being conformed to the world rather than actively influencing the world (cf. Rom. 12:1, 2).

The other epigram deals with the tragic one-sided development of a people that is "a cake not turned." The home policy is as serious as the foreign policy. Ephraim is like a neglected cake lying on hot coals that has been burned to a cinder on one side while the other is still raw. Israel is wholly unfit for anything. George Adam Smith says: "Want of thoroughness and equable effort was Israel's besetting sin, and it told on all sides of his life. How better describe a half-fed people, a half-cultured society, a half-lived religion, a half-hearted policy, than by a half-baked scone?" [23]

Hosea is emphasizing their unconsciousness of these dangerous symptoms. It is a sad day when a man is not conscious of his distance from God, his dissipating tendencies, his poor development, his gradual decadence, and his glaring sins that are so clearly visible through God's eyes. Signs of senile decay go unheeded. In a silly fashion he counts his money and congratulates himself on his successes without realizing that his distinctive virtue has been dissipated.

Accompanying this decadence will always be an assumption of easygoing superiority. The man will have such a lofty opinion of himself that he will not feel any need for a turn-

[23] *Ibid.*, p. 273.

ing to God. He spends his time, his energy and his mind in foolish pursuits that leave him helpless and undone.

> *Woe to them! for they have wandered from me . . .*
> *they have rebelled against me . . . they have spoken*
> *lies against me . . . they have not cried to me with*
> *their hearts . . . against me they think only evil.*
> (7:13-15.)

What an indictment of God's people! For years they have rendered lip service and only when afraid of drought and crop failure have they called on Him. They use the senseless means which the pagan neighbors used to placate a god whom they misunderstand. They claim that they are justified in turning to other lovers since Yahweh has refused to help them in return for their service. They are told that their real action has been wandering, rebelling, speaking lies, failing to pray to Him, and devising evil of Him. We need not wonder that God was ready to abandon them to exile.

> *For they sow the wind and they will reap the whirl-*
> *wind. Israel is swallowed up; now have they become*
> *among the nations like a vessel for which there is*
> *no use.* (8:7.)

The results of sin are like the power of gravity. The speed of the fall increases in ratio to the distance. The mighty storm comes as a natural consequence of the early sowing of a gentle zephyr. The day of reaping is the day of suffering. Unforeseen terrors are in store for the one who has carelessly plunged into sin. This beautiful vessel that gave so much promise in its youth has now become utterly useless because it has allowed itself to become swallowed up by the peoples of Canaan. This verse describes Israel's history for more than two thousand years. It makes our heart bleed to look back upon the tragedies and sufferings of God's chosen people (cf. 9:17).

> *Like grapes in the wilderness I found Israel; like*
> *the first fruit on the fig tree, in its first season, I saw*
> *your fathers; but they came to Baal-peor and conse-*
> *crated themselves to shame and became as abomin-*
> *able as that which they loved.* (9:10.)

Hosea describes God recounting His first pictures of Israel in the honeymoon days under the pale desert moon. He thinks of them as unspoiled, fresh, fragrant, attractive as His eye first fastened itself upon them in the wilderness. He lingers lovingly over the early history of His chosen people. What promise! What precious fruit! Memories of the purity and freshness of His bride throng His soul.

But the sad chapter follows rapidly upon the romance of the honeymoon. At the very first shrine of Canaan they had polluted themselves, becoming like the abominable thing which they worshiped. The object of their immoral worship infected their own lives.

As a result *Ephraim* (which means fruitful) will be barren and bring forth no fruit. Thus he says *"Fruitful* shall be *fruitless."* Barrenness is the result of an impure and polluted worship.

> *Sow to yourselves righteousness, reap the fruit of*
> *love; break up your fallow ground; for it is time to*
> *seek Yahweh.* (10:12)

Israel is in for some rough plowing. Instead of soft, easy, effortless living and worship she must learn the sterner discipline. The ground must be broken deep. The clods must be turned up to the sun and rain. In order to enjoy God's grace, Israel must change her evil habits and get right with God so that He can change the lives of her people.

Instead of wickedness and lies she must be willing to sow righteousness and godliness. The people are reminded that there is still time to begin. They are allowed free choice in the matter. The choice is urgent.

When Israel was a child, then I loved him, And out of Egypt I called him to be my son. Yet it was I who taught Ephraim to walk; taking them by the arms, but they knew not that I healed them. (11:1, 3.)

Again we get a glimpse into the tender heart of God who is pictured as a loving Father who has had His heart broken into bits by ingratitude, impurity and callous ignorance. Looking beyond these heart-rending experiences He remembers the days of the Exodus. T. H. Robinson says there are few more beautiful or appealing pictures in literature than that of the father teaching his child to walk.[24]

God passed over the strong, rich, powerful boys of the earth in the selection of His favorite son upon whom should come all the covenant blessings. He chose a young, weak unattractive slave boy from the land of Egypt to be the object of His love and rich blessings. He says: *"I began, I learned to love him."* God loved him and called him and led him and healed him.

That dear boy was trained with affectionate care. His little feet were taught to step (*walk*). When he grew tired he was taken up into the strong arms of a Father. This is a great picture of fatherhood in any age.

In spite of all this tender solicitude and care the boy has broken the Father's heart. All the love has been lavished in vain. As a result exile and slaughter are inevitable. Sin has done its destructive work and nothing short of suffering can now save Israel. In it all there must be a subconscious realization that they are not their own but they are bought with a price and must be lifted by an eternal hope that shall not be denied.

How can I give thee up, Ephraim?
How can I let thee go, Israel?

[24] *Prophecy and the Prophets*, p. 77. Used by permission of the publishers Charles Scribner's Sons.

*My heart is turned within me, my compassions are
kindled together.* (11:8.)

Once more the Father voices His undying love for His
chosen ones. Tenderly He expresses His deepest love. How
can a Father deliberately send His precious child to certain
destruction? How can He allow one whom He has loved
from the cradle days to go into a horrible exile? Geo. A.
Smith says: "Yet God is God, and though prophecy fail He
will attempt His love once more. There follows the greatest
passage in Hosea—deepest if not highest of his book—the
breaking forth of that exhaustless mercy of the Most High
which no sin of man can bar back nor wear out." [25]
This verse has been called "The Remorse of God," for
through it the reader is allowed to see the divine heart burst-
ing with love and tenderness for the wayward child. It is
asking too much of a great Father to demand that His
favorite son be driven off into destruction. Surely, Ephraim
will hear and have his heart melted by such a plea.

*Return, O Israel, to Yahweh, thy God; For thou
hast fallen by thine iniquity. Take with you words,
and return to Yahweh. Say to him, "remove altogether iniquity, and receive us graciously and we
will render the fruit of our lips."* (14:2.)

Yahweh's earnest pleading continues. Again the prophet
pictures the tender love of God for His wayward children
who have caused Him so much grief. He wants them to know
that the door is still open for them to return to their own
Father's house. They have failed to find God in the past
because their approach has been wrong. Bulls and goats and
offerings have not been sufficient. A mechanical observance
of ritual requirements could not avail. He begs Israel to
learn from her bitter experience the folly of separation from
God and to come back home.

Ibid., p. 297.

Briefly and clearly he sets forth the proper method of approach. God wants confessions and vows that come from the heart. When a penitent soul comes into the presence of God his sin becomes hateful to him. He feels the need of grace, and cries, "remove iniquity altogether." The confession of sin will bring full forgiveness from Yahweh who loves with such a passionate love. Israel promises (verse 2) that she will no longer put her trust in the help of alien armies. Assyria and Egypt are powerless to help. The idols that have been manufactured are equally impotent. She will adjure all human help and cast herself on the mercy of Yahweh who is able and willing to deliver.

Yahweh says:

I will heal their backsliding, I will love them freely: for my anger is turned away from them. (14:4.)

What a beautiful promise! How gracious is the response of their Father! For a long season His great heart has been full of love but their sins have kept Him from bestowing rich blessings. Now every barrier is out of the way, every sin is confessed and Yahweh opens the floodgate to let the torrent of love sweep over to fill and bless penitent children. Amazing grace will find a way to restore them to their place as sons, to heal their sick souls, to set them in paths of righteousness, and to reveal to them the depths of the divine love. His wrath has vanished, His forgiveness is complete, His grace knows no bounds, His love will continue to pour itself out in an unending stream.

The picture that follows is full of fresh beauty and fragrance and hope for the restored people who, in their new relationship, will rejoice continually in the love and mercy of God. No longer will they yearn for the idols and the old lovers. They are to be happy in His presence always.

PRACTICAL LESSONS OF PERMANENT VALUE

1. Nothing is able to quench God's love.
2. God suffers intense pain when men desert Him.
3. The sacredness and sanctity of the marriage relation.
4. The tragic consequence of heeding unworthy teachers.
5. In God's plan there can be no double standard of morality.
6. Sin destroys the nerve that enables men to make moral distinctions.
7. Divorce is not a solution. It is merely an effort to escape.
8. Worship cannot please God until the worshiper comes in the right spirit.
9. A nation declines rapidly when its leaders become corrupt.
10. There is real danger of becoming like those with whom we associate.
11. Genuine repentance will bring forgiveness and full restoration of God's favor.
12. Inward corruption in a nation is more dangerous to its existence than external enemies.
13. The root sin from which all others spring is unfaithfulness to Yahweh.

''' ISAIAH '''

THE LAST FORTY YEARS OF THE EIGHTH CENTURY PRODUCED great men but the greatest of these was the prophet Isaiah. Amos and Hosea were preaching in the Northern Kingdom and Micah was active in the Southern Kingdom with Isaiah. We can learn much of God and His purpose for the world from a careful study of the background, the prophet, and his book.

THE WORLD IN ISAIAH'S DAY

The political picture reveals a world stretching itself for a titanic struggle. World forces were girding for a battle for supremacy. Uzziah and Jeroboam II were closing out prosperous reigns that brought peace, plenty and extravagance to the leading citizens. Surrounding nations had been so weak that almost no opposition had been encountered. Jotham, Ahaz and Hezekiah followed Uzziah on the throne of Judah. Through these years the statesman prophet preached in Jerusalem.

In 745 B.C. Assyria came to life in a vigorous way under the dynamic leadership of Tiglath Pileser. His power was soon felt in Palestine. Menahem paid a heavy tribute to buy him off. He came back in 734 B.C. at the call of the weak Ahaz to drive ruthlessly over Syria and the Northern Kingdom. Damascus fell in 732 B.C. and Israel was destroyed with the exception of the city of Samaria which defied capture until 722 B.C. Ahaz became subject to Assyria with little real independence left.

Shalmanezer (727-722 B.C.) began the siege of Samaria and Sargon II (722-705 B.C.) completed the capture by taking the people away into captivity. Sennacherib (705-681 B.C.) proved the painful thorn in the side of Judah. His terrible invasion of the Westland in 701 B.C. was one of the classic invasions of

83

history. All the cities of Palestine were taken except Jerusalem and its destruction was prevented only by the divine
intervention that left 185,000 Assyrian soldiers dead. These
four Assyrian monarchs played a big part in the drama of
history enacted during Isaiah's day.

In Syria Rezin proved the most powerful of the kings but
he was killed in the fall of Damascus in 732 B.C. His alliance
with Pekah of Israel brought on the fatal Assyrian invasion
and the end of Syria as an independent power.

In Babylon definite trends in the direction of world do-
minion were noticeable although a hundred years were to
pass before Babylonian supremacy. Isaiah predicts the day of
her power. Merodach Baladan was ruling from 721-710 B.C.

In Egypt the twenty-third dynasty held sway during the
early days of Isaiah's ministry. The twenty-fourth and
twenty-fifth dynasties followed before his death.

In Rome Romulus and Remus were in the midst of the
picture. The traditional founding of the city is set at 753 B.C.
only a few years after the birth of the prophet Isaiah.

In Greece the close of the Mycaean age was at hand and
the rise of the city states was beginning. Sparta and Athens
came into being.

Social conditions. A government-fostered prosperity held
sway in the land. There was a rich class and a poor class with
the customary chasm between them. Abuses, resentment,
unrest, class feeling and profiteering were in evidence on all
sides. Land-grabbing was one of the gravest problems of the
day. Original owners lost their homes while unscrupulous
men, who used extortion and eviction to gain their wicked
ends, became the owners. The corrupt city government and
the covetous judiciary made life miserable for the poor of the
land. Luxury and idleness and indifference to the wants of
others added to the suffering of many and to the worthlessness of those who were prosperous. The drink evil added its
toll of sorrow and distress and want.

Religious conditions. The people of Israel had been

brought into Palestine to give a religious quality and a message to the nations round about. Instead of playing this role they had come down to the same level as their neighbors and had become importers rather than exporters. Baalism had done its worst. Superstitions, customs from the East, and the deadly worship of Moloch broke down any spiritual impressions they might have had. There was very little religious depth, the moral fibre was gone, ethical standards were low. Prophets were too busy with strong drink to give attention to the spiritual welfare of the people. They had no message of value even if they had wanted to help spiritually. The women were coarse, sensual, drunken and thoughtless. The task of a prophet was a difficult one. How could he cope with such problems and lead such people to spiritual understanding?

THE MAN OF GOD

The son of Amoz was born in Jerusalem about 760 B.C. when Amos was on his expedition to Israel. His active ministry began about 740 B.C. in the year king Uzziah died. For forty years he preached in his native city, giving to kings, princes and people the burning messages from God. We may think of him as a young aristocrat from a princely line who had access to the court and high standing with the people of Jerusalem. He was married as early as 734 B.C. and had at least two sons.

His equipment and training were the best that his age afforded. In body, in mind, in temperament, in personality, he was superbly endowed with the qualities that fitted him for highest usefulness. His intimate knowledge of the city, the kingdom, the surrounding nations, and the history of the world fitted him to interpret the meaning of all the movements of peoples in the light of God's will. It is highly probable that he was influenced by contact with Amos, Hosea and Micah. The greatest influence in his life was the compelling grip of God's hand upon him that kept him constantly at the task of preaching.

His call was a never-to-be-forgotten experience. It came in the year of the tragic death of the grand old king. In an hour of meditation he saw God on a throne, robed in splendor, in holiness, in glory. He could never be the same again. Instantly his eyes turned upon himself and he realized that he was unclean, unworthy, needy and undone. The cry of repentance brought healing, and his eyes then beheld a sinning, needy world calling out for help. His response was immediate, *"Here am I, send me."* He was accepted, commissioned and empowered to go forth as Yahweh's representative to the wicked people. Hardships, perils and disappointments awaited him, but in God's strength he would be victorious.

His ministry. For forty years Isaiah spent his life preaching, predicting deliverances, writing prophecies and counseling kings. These experiences were made beautiful by a dignity, a personal magnetism, a clear faith, and a genuine love for Yahweh that continually called out his best efforts. Through stormy days and in the sunlit seasons he was the man of the hour. God's prophet was the greatest man of his generation.

As a statesman he has no equal among the prophets. When the weak Ahaz trembled before the approach of Pekah and Rezin it was the prophet who appealed to him to put his trust in God for help rather than call in Tiglath Pileser from Nineveh. His wisdom and courage grew out of his faith in God, but he revealed a grasp of the principles of which true statesmen are made. When the princes of Judah determined to break the alliance with Assyria to cast their lot with Egypt, it was the preacher who cautioned against the suicidal policy. When the mighty Sennacherib ran roughshod over all of Palestine and broke the power of an Egyptian army, it was the statesman preacher who counseled faith in God even in that disastrous hour. No other living man could have been so sure of the security of the Holy City. In addition he predicted the complete overthrow of the proud Assyrian. His faith in God gave him the basis for such wise counsel, but his keen statesmanlike mind was used to an advantage. When

Hezekiah foolishly showed off all his treasures and military equipment to the men from Babylon, it was Isaiah, the statesman, who rebuked him for his folly and predicted the coming of the Babylonian army to destroy the kingdom of Judah. More than one hundred years were to elapse before that fateful day, but even though Assyria was at the zenith of her glory as a world power, the true statesman could see the coming world conqueror.

As a preacher of social righteousness he had no equal among the prophets. He had deep convictions, kingly courage, clear vision, spiritual intuition, and unusual power in driving home the truth. His love for righteousness grew out of his keen appreciation of the absolute righteousness of God and the divine abhorrence of sin. Since he was not a member of the peasant group he cannot be accused of being selfishly biased in favor of the poor. His righteous indignation burned at the very thought of injustice, cruelty, oppression, dishonesty and immorality. Not once does he elect to condone unrighteous acts in any individual. Kings, judges, princes and merchants are all chastised by his stinging rebuke. With his head in the clouds and his feet on the earth he spent his days trying to help sinful people see God as he knew Him, hate sin as He hated it, and turn as devotedly to the work of blessing human hearts. His thoughts were practical, his judgments accurate, his vision clear, his zeal aflame, his purpose large and his enthusiasm unbounded. Dignified oratory poured forth from a pure heart with peculiar directness and uncanny effectiveness.

As a spiritual giant Isaiah stands as the loftiest peak among the mountains. From the day of his vision in the Temple he possessed a heavenly glow and a spiritual depth that set him apart from his contemporaries. From his place as a contrite sinner begging for mercy he became a commissioned saint with the breath of heaven about him. He walked with God, and that divine fellowship did something for him that is indescribable. From intimate touch with God he was able to

make others sense something of His infinite loveliness and
His precious nearness as well as the transcendent qualities
that set Him so far above men. The deep spirituality of the
prophet gave his words added meaning as they came to
human ears. With all his heart he hated uncleanness and
loved holiness. He spent his life trying to get Israel to become acquainted with God and His word and to trust implicitly in God's guidance. Surely that is a worthy aim for
the men of our day!

THE BOOK

The sixty-six chapters in our present volume are clearly
divided into three separate books (1-39; 40-55; 56-66). How
many of these chapters are from the pen of Isaiah the son of
Amoz? Could he have written material that announces the
return from captivity after the campaigns of Cyrus? What
about a deutero-Isaiah or a trito-Isaiah? A study of these
questions would take us too far afield. The general consensus
of opinion is that we have at least two authors and perhaps
three. The view would give to Isaiah the majority of 1-39
and attribute chapters 40-66 to one or two later disciples of
the great prophet. Perhaps we shall never know the truth of
the matter. If Isaiah did write 40-66 it was necessary for him
to change his standing point from 700 B.C. to 540 B.C. when
the Exile was ready to end. Under the influence of the Spirit
could he pick himself up and journey one hundred and fifty
years to a new point of vantage and begin again without any
word to make the transition intelligible to the reader?

According to the canons of criticism a prophet speaks only
to his own generation and therefore it would be out of the
question to think of writing down a message to lie quietly
by for a century and a half before it could be applied. The
style and language and religious ideas of 40-66 contrast
strongly with the undisputed writings of Isaiah. Cyrus is
named as the deliverer from Babylonian captivity when in
Isaiah's day the Babylonian supremacy has not even begun.
Cyrus, the great Persian leader, is pictured as already on his

way to help Israel. The author presents him as a definite proof that former predictions are now being fulfilled and that God keeps His word.

It should be said that there is no reference in 40-66 to indicate the identity of the author. No claim is made for Isaiah or anyone else. When all the arguments are arrayed on each side of the question we are still left without conclusive proof. The reader is left to choose for himself, knowing that if he accepts the theory of two or three authors, he may still value the material as highly as he could if he were convinced that Isaiah wrote it all. It is God's revelation to men and as such we accept it, treasure it, agree to search its passages, learn its messages, and be guided by its truths.

The contents. Taking the book as a whole it falls into the following clearly defined divisions:

I

1-12 Rebukes and promises directed at the people of Judah
13-23 Prophecies concerning foreign nations
24-35 Prophecies of general judgment on Judah and Jerusalem
36-39 A historical section dealing with Hezekiah and Sennacherib

II

40-48 Genuine comfort for the exiles
49-55 The Servant of Yahweh
56-66 The future glory of Israel

PREACHING VALUES

No book in the Old Testament provides such rich treasures of preaching material for the minister who will get into the spirit of Isaiah and present the material with the abandon of a prophet. Great themes present themselves for treatment. Chapters such as the first, sixth, fortieth, forty-ninth, fiftieth, fifty-third and fifty-fifth will delight the heart of the expositor. Scores of briefer texts clamor for recognition and use. The picture of the Messiah is clearly drawn with an ever deepening beauty and attractiveness. A challenging social emphasis is unfolded in sermons that reveal God's love for the underprivileged, the oppressed and the neglected. Hopeful promises along the way remind us of the mercy that God has provided for those who love Him enough to commit their way to Him. Severe warnings grip us as we begin to turn into forbidden paths. Let us approach its pages with reverence and appreciation, praying for His guidance all the way.

Some great texts.

> *Sons I have brought up and exalted, but they have rebelled against me. The ox knows . . . Israel does not know. The whole head is sick, the whole heart is faint . . . I am sated with the burnt offerings . . . When you make many prayers I will not hear. Come now let us reason together . . . Though your sins be as scarlet they shall be as white as snow.* (1:2-20.)

This "great arraignment" is a terrific word to rebellious sinners who were breaking the heart of God with their sins.

2-4   The soliloquy of a brokenhearted father. Ingratitude and rebellion bring tragic heartaches.

5-9   A picture of present miseries brought on by sin.

10-15   The utter worthlessness of rites and ceremonies and offerings and prayers.

16-17   A fervent exhortation. "Take a good bath and mend your ways."

18   An earnest invitation and a golden promise.

19-20   The divine alternative.

Some one else has suggested these four points:

2-9   Thoughtlessness

10-17   Formalism

18-23 Pardon
24-31 Redemption

> *Many peoples shall go and say:*
> *Come let us go up to the mountain of Yahweh that*
> *he may teach us . . . that we may walk in His paths;*
> *for out of Zion goes forth instruction . . . He will*
> *judge . . . give decisions . . . they will learn war no*
> *more.* (2:2-4.)

This beautiful poem, found also in Mic. 4:1-3, is one of the choice gems of all literature. Whether written by Micah or Isaiah or some earlier author matters little, for we find in it a bit of timeless beauty, made exquisite by the very air of heaven. Call it the dream of an idealist if you like but recognize in it the ideal program of God for His chosen people. He wants them to make their way eagerly to the place where He is teaching so that they may catch and understand and translate into living all the riches of His instruction. Disputes, misunderstandings, arguments and other differences will melt away in the light of the Teacher who reveals His truth to them. Wars will be out of the question when nations and individuals submit all their differences to the divine Arbiter. God's plan for His people includes turning away from worldly teachings, sitting at the feet of the great Teacher, walking in His paths, and putting into practice all His teachings.

> *In that day . . . he that is left in Zion . . . shall*
> *be called holy . . . when the Lord shall have washed*
> *away the filth of Zion's daughters . . . by a blast of*
> *judgment and by a blast of burning.* (4:2-6.)

If the picture in the second chapter is the dream of an idealist who sees a glorious future for God's people and the picture in 2:6-4:1 is the dark realistic presentation of a tragic failure, this text furnishes the revelation of a new glory seen through the eyes of a chastened idealist. He is conscious of all the sin and filth and ugliness of Jerusalem but he knows of the purging, cleansing, purifying fires of God's judgment. When God gets through with His drastic purging the city will be clean. Purity and holiness will characterize her citizens who have been made holy by His touch. Even sinful, defiled, filthy men and women can be redeemed and made clean by His touch.

> *I will sing of my beloved, a love-song concerning his vineyard . . .*
> *He digged it and cleared it of stones and planted it with choice vines . . . built a tower . . . hewed out a wine-vat in it and he waited . . . but it bore stinking grapes.* (5:1-7.)

This love song almost breaks the heart of one who looks intently upon the figure of the patient, expectant, sacrificial planter who is so poignantly disappointed. Isaiah has used his keenest faculties in presenting all the angles of the tragic picture. Careful selection, diligent preparation, wise planting and ardent wishing characterize his activities. In return for all this effort and sacrifice only stinking, worthless grapes appear. Quickly the preacher turns the application to his neighbors in Judah. Yahweh's heart is weeping because He looked for justice and righteousness but found bloodshed and the frantic cry of distress. What a harvest to reap in return for all the love and sacrifice expended!

> *I saw the Lord . . . Holy, holy, holy is Yahweh of Hosts . . . "Woe is me" . . . "I am a man of unclean lips" . . . He touched my mouth . . . "Thy sin is forgiven" . . . "Whom shall I send?" "Here am I; send me." "Go and say." (6:1-13.)*

The secret of Isaiah's tremendous power in the world is unveiled for us in this picture of his experience with God. Even as Paul always looked back to that hour on the Damascus road so does Isaiah date his peculiar effectiveness from the vision of God. In that brief account we see conviction, contrition, conversion, confession, cleansing, and consecration. Some preacher has called it "the 'woe' of conviction, the 'lo' of cleansing, and the 'go' of service." In it is clearly pictured the four steps in a soul's experience.

1. *Revelation*—He saw God in His majesty and might.
2. *Prostration*—He saw his own unworthiness and his distance from God.
3. *Purification*—God's cleansing touch brought full purification.
4. *Consecration*—Without reservation he offered himself on God's altar for service.

The people who walked in darkness have seen a great light . . .
For to us a child is born, to us a son is given . . . his name . . .
Wonderful Counselor, Mighty God, Everlasting Father, Prince of Peace. (9:1-6.)

Darkness, distress, anguish and gloom will be dispelled and God's glorious light will take its place in the world, *for* the gift of heaven to earth is to come in the person of a holy Child. What a transformation His coming is to make! Even Isaiah at the distance of seven hundred years is able to describe something of the glory of it. Divine wisdom, divine might, divine fatherhood, and divine peace are to come as a result of His reign on the earth. These four pairs of names for the Messiah emphasize His divinity. The coming King is wise, is mighty, is to be a guardian of His people, and will bring into the world a heavenly peace.

Will come forth a shoot from the stock of Jesse . . .
the Spirit of Yahweh will rest upon him, the spirit of wisdom . . . understanding . . . counsel . . . might . . . knowledge . . . fear of Yahweh . . . and right-

> *eousness the girdle of his loins and faithfulness . . .*
> *his reins . . . for the earth will be full of the knowl-*
> *edge of Yahweh.* (11:1-5, 9.)

This portrait of the Messiah presents Him as the Ideal Judge solicitous for the rights of the weak and helpless ones of the earth. He will see to it that all men everywhere find justice meted out. This man from Jesse's stock will have wisdom, might, and will delight in God. God's Spirit will endow Him with the qualities of soul and mind that will fit Him to have human souls and destinies entrusted to His care. (Cf. also 16:5 and 32:1, 2.)

> *I give thee thanks, O Yahweh; for thou wast angry*
> *with me, but thine anger is turned away . . . God*
> *is my deliverance; I will trust and not be afraid . . .*
> *Yahweh is my strength and song; and he has become*
> *my salvation.* (12:1, 2.)

This is an oasis in the chapters of this section of Isaiah. Joy reigns in his heart and he breaks forth in grateful acknowledgment. He is sure now that God's anger has passed and that the divine sunlight is flooding the earth about him. He is now constrained to declare his faith in God. No more fear will afflict him for he has a grip on God that makes fear fly away and shouts of joy and praise flow from his lips. In the light of God's signal deliverance he will pledge his best self in loyal service.

> *He will destroy death forever;*
> *The Lord Yahweh will wipe tears from all faces.*
> (25:8.)

What a great prophecy of God's plan to swallow up death and make eternity glorious for all believers! Only in Him do we have any hope beyond the grave. He can redeem human beings by His own sacrificial offering and provide eternal security for each of them. Tears will be quickly brushed away and faces will be lighted with His radiance when we see the glories He has provided for those who fear Him. Such a hope should constrain us to give ourselves in devoted service to Him. (Cf. also 26:19.)

> *Thou wilt keep him in perfect peace whose mind is*
> *stayed on thee, because he trusteth in thee.* (26:3.)

The psychiatrist reaches for this verse when he finds need for a substantial hold for one who has been dominated by fear. What a joy it is to find it and have it available! How rich it is in strength-giving aid! When we grope madly for an antidote for fear why not try this verse? This is the one perfect way to the conquest of fear. Let us begin by putting it to the test. Do I trust fully in Him? Does fear hinder me from a full, rich, abundant life? Fear of life, fear of death, fear of eternity, need not wreck me. Remember this text.

> *Comfort ye, comfort ye my people . . .*
> *Speak to the heart of Jerusalem and proclaim to*
> *her.* (40:1, 2.)

We recognize this as God's word to a crowd of people who have been exiled from home and native land. He is speaking to His people a message of hope and cheer in that dark hour of exile. It is enough for them to know that God really cares. The distress of His people has grieved the great heart of God. Our greatest source of strength is to know just this message of comfort. These verses sound forth the voice of *Grace*. The proclamation of forgiveness is God's answer to drooping spirits. Yahweh is moving in force for His people. He is a God who works. He wants His people to have a direct word driven to the heart that assures divine redemption. Israel's full pardon is at hand. What a message of peace, of mercy, of grace, of eternal pardon!

> *Grass withers, flowers fade: but the Word of our*
> *God stands forever.* (40:8.)

In verses 3-11 the author tells us how the promise is fulfilled. The voice of grace is followed by the voice of prophecy and then by the voice of faith. Here the objective reality of God's redemption is revealed. In the midst of this theological discussion we run into this side remark that lights up the whole paragraph. He claims that grass fades or withers but that Yahweh's Word has an eternal quality that reveals something of His pledge and an earnest of that divine redemption.

The Lord Yahweh comes as a mighty One, his arm
ruling for Him . . .
He will feed his flock like a shepherd,
He will gather the lambs in His arms, and carry
them in his bosom, and will gently lead those that
give suck. (40:10, 11.)

The Judge and King is coming! He is mighty in power, filled with wisdom and yet gentle and considerate in dealing with those who need help. Yahweh has all of these qualities as He comes to rescue His people who have suffered so sorely. With strong arms, keen eyes, and tender care He will deal with His chosen ones. These pictures of God are still true and would help us in a tremendous way if we could see Him with power and with tenderness seeking to help all people. He is the loving Father presented by our Lord and Saviour.

To whom then will ye liken God? (40:12-26.)

The prophet launches forth to give a picture of the Incomparable One in contrast with the helpless idols that lie beneath Him. His unique character is revealed. He is the infinite One when compared with the created ones, when compared with other gods, and when compared with the stars. His sovereignty and omnipotence are clearly pictured in language that defies description. Brilliant monotheism is clearly presented to us. The eternal One has all of this power and yet He knows each of His sheep by name and cares for each one individually.

*Yahweh is an everlasting God, the Creator of the
ends of the earth. He wearies not and faints not; his
understanding is unsearchable. He gives vigor to
the weary . . . Youths may faint and grow weary and
young men may utterly fail: But those who wait on
Yahweh renew their strength; they mount up with
wings like eagles; they run and are not weary; they
walk, and do not faint. (40:27-31.)*

Following the argument given in the preceding paragraph
the author goes on with a thrilling application. He represents
Yahweh as acquainted with Israel's misery. He never faints
or grows weary. He sustains the faint and the wearied ones.
He can be trusted. Why not wait on Him and let Him bring
joy and security and peace? "Fly, run, walk!" This description of human experience reveals, not an anticlimax, but a
real climax. God will make it possible for each individual to
walk patiently in the way under His leadership.

*Fear not, for I am with thee; be not dismayed, for I
am thy God. I strengthen thee; yea, I help thee.*
(41:8-10.)

These are comforting words to Israel who has been chosen
as God's servant and who sees in the coming events shadows
that will bring intense sufferings. Exodus 19:6 tells us of the
choice of Israel as the servant of Yahweh. Many years have
passed and she still lacks much in measuring up to God's
ideal for her. This promise was designed to help keep alive
in her breast the knowledge of God's love for her and His
willingness to continue needed help. The coming of Cyrus is
proof that Yahweh presides over the destinies of all nations.

*Bring forward your case, says Yahweh. Declare the
things that are to come hereafter that we may know
that ye are gods; yea, do something, good or bad.*
(41:21-23.)

Yahweh is superior to dumb animals in that He can pre-dict the future. Cyrus is presented as God's coming repre-sentative who will perform wonders in the divine power. These poor, helpless pieces of wood cannot be depended upon for any help in the hour of need. With keen irony He calls on the idols to do something—just anything, to prove their identity as gods. Yahweh is making His predictions and will stake His honor upon the fulfillment of the prophecies.

> *Behold my Servant . . . my chosen in whom my soul delights . . . He will not shout . . . a bruised reed he will not break . . . He will not be quenched or be crushed, till he have set judgment in the earth.*
> (42:1-9.)

In this first of the four Servant poems the author describes the character of the Servant of Yahweh. God speaks about Him and then speaks to Him. The Servant is divinely chosen, called, sustained, anointed, equipped, and He delights the heart of God. His character, His method, His work and His steadfast faith are pictured. He is gentle, merciful, patient and persevering in dealing with weak individuals who need consideration. He is made powerful by Yahweh and is endowed with a two-fold mission to restore the Jews and bring light to the Gentiles. He is to be priest, prophet, teacher, guide, and deliverer. God is responsible for the suc-cess of the work but He puts the load upon the willing shoul-ders of His servant.

> *Fear not, for I have redeemed thee; I have called thee by name, thou are mine. When thou passest through the waters I will be with thee; and through the rivers, they shall not overflow thee: When thou goest through the fire thou shalt not be burned.*
> (43:1-5.)

Here is God's unchanging promise **to anyone** who is beginning to fear or who is being called upon to pass through dark waters of grief or suffering. How good He is to give us the comfort of these words! We belong to Him. He has ransomed us. He will be with us in flaming fires, in raging storms, in overflowing floods of waters. He is personally interested and able to save unto the uttermost. "Hallelujah, what a Saviour!"

> *Is there a God besides me? . . . Those who fashion images are all of them chaos . . . He kindles a fire and bakes bread, yea, he makes a god and worships it . . . falls down to it, and worships and prays to it. (44:8-20.)*

Again the contrast between the Living God and helpless idols is presented. How pathetic the picture! How tragic the realization! In striking contrast to these lifeless wooden idols the eternal God forgives and redeems, He lives, He moves, He predicts future events, He saves his people.

> *Turn to me and be ye saved all the ends of the earth; for I am God, there is none else. (45:22.)*

The victory of Cyrus will cause the heathen to know of God's deity and many will turn to Him as a result of the signal deliverance. In the light of this prediction he gives an invitation to all men of all nations to come to the One who can save. The message on theology is linked to a great missionary invitation. Since Yahweh is a covenant-keeping God the individual can count on Him to do the saving. When the eye is turned upon Him the heart will go out in faith to Him. Salvation will come to him who believes.

> *Yahweh called me . . . made my mouth like a sharp sword . . . hid me . . . covered me . . . said to me, "Thou art my Servant, Israel, in whom I will glorify myself. I will set thee to be the light of the nations." (49:1-6.)*

In this second Servant poem the Servant speaks as a prophet. He has recognized His mission to exhort, rouse, and extricate the rest of the nation. He must glorify God by speech and by suffering. He tells of His call, His preparation and the divine equipment. He is a "polished arrow," "hidden," ready for instant use. He is the chief weapon in God's plans, kept for the hour of deepest need. In view of the signal honor conferred upon Him, there is a strange despondency apparent. God rewards Him in that peculiar hour with a new work. He must go to the Gentiles with the message of His Father. He is assured of future successes because God is still in love with His people and cannot forget them. They must be restored. Such an assurance calls for a new song.

> *Zion said: "Yahweh has forsaken me." Can a woman forget her suckling child? Yea, she may forget, yet will I not forget thee. Behold, I have graven thee upon the palms of my hands; thy walls are continually before me. (49:14-16.)*

All through the ages men have complained that God forgets them. Suffering or want or sorrow may make them feel neglected and self-pity very often results. Yahweh is quick to deny the charge. He has put the individual's name on His very hands and a picture before Him so that He is continually conscious of each face. It is comforting to know that we are the objects of His love and care and that He is thinking about us every moment (cf. Ps. 40:17).

> *Yahweh has given me a disciple's tongue that I may know how to lift the weary with words. Morning by morning he wakens my ear to hear as a disciple. The Lord Yahweh has opened my ear, and I was not rebellious . . . I gave my back to the smiters . . . I hid not my face from shame and spitting . . . I have set my face like a flint, and I know that I shall not be ashamed. (50:4-9.)*

The third Servant poem gives us a picture of the Servant speaking of His devotion to His work.

50:4. He is *taught by Yahweh* that He may teach others. He comforts, sustains and strengthens.

   5. *Filial obedience.* In the supreme test He does not fail. He knows the difficulties but He refuses to be disloyal to His Teacher.

   6. *A willing Sufferer.* He is challenged by shame, insults, cruelty and pain. His back is to be torn and bruised while insults are heaped upon Him, but He suffers willingly and obediently.

   7. *An inflexible resolve.* This courageous conqueror faces the future resolutely and with steadfastness because He is leaning upon the Lord Yahweh. The Servant is certain of victory because He has all the resources of heaven at His disposal.

   8. *A bold challenge.* Suddenly He challenges anyone to stand up against Him with an accusation because He has His advocate on His side.

   9. *Certain triumph.* The Servant is still the unconvicted One. Accusations are utterly useless because His eternal God is on His side.

Awake, awake, put on thy strength, O Zion; Put on thy beautiful garments, O Jerusalem. (52:1, 2.)

What a challenge to drooping hearts! Years of suffering and distress and loneliness have left her in a deplorable condition. Yahweh's call to her is one that is calculated to cause joy to rise in her heart. Nothing will be as fitting as a joyous response to His request. Every little church is a Zion and should be thrilled by the call of God to put on her beautiful garments and go forth to praise and worship. Each church would be a happier group and would be more enthusiastic in the work of God if the words of this text were put into actual use.

He was wounded for our transgressions, He was crushed for our iniquities: The chastisement of our peace was upon him; and through his stripes healing came to us. All we like sheep had gone astray; we had turned every man to his own way; But Yahweh made to light on him the iniquity of us all.
(52:13-53:12.)

These five matchless stanzas of the fourth Servant poem are the Mount Everest of Messianic Prophecy. The Servant's destiny, career, suffering, submission and reward, are pictured in these strophes.

52:13-15   The Servant, from the highest exaltation, is caused to suffer humiliation on His way to even higher exaltation again. His suffering is to issue in glory. He shall startle many nations.

53:1-3   The humiliation and suffering of a Redeemer. The figures are so startling that one is compelled to look on Him.

53:4-6   The meaning of His suffering is seen in vicarious, substitutionary atonement that results in full redemption. The pure for the unholy and the righteous substitute for the sinner. He was wounded, bruised, chastised, pierced, plagued, crushed—not for His own sins, but for ours. He bore on His own person the sins of the world. Yahweh is a forgiving God who provided this holy Substitute.

53:7-9   The sinless Substitute suffers silently for the sins of others. Silently He submits to the will of God. His innocence is affirmed. His death is voluntarily accepted without a whimper or complaint. The sinless One is condemned while the guilty one goes free. The Lamb of God makes possible the matchless salvation.

53:10-12　God's purpose fulfilled as the Sufferer is exalted to the highest place after the hour of deepest humiliation. God willed it. His death satisfied the Father, satisfied justice, satisfied the sinner and the Sufferer. His purpose was two-fold: to bring many sons to glory and to make the Servant the supreme Priest and Intercessor. He lives, He reigns, He intercedes. He suffered, was rejected, betrayed, killed that He might reign victoriously. "Hallelujah! What a Saviour!"

Enlarge the place of thy tent, and let them stretch forth the curtains of thy habitations; spare not; lengthen thy cords and strengthen thy stakes. (54:2.)

God wanted redeemed Zion to make ready for a rich consignment of blessings. Her puny warehouses were inadequate and her little heart was not able to appreciate the gifts that He wished to lavish upon the city. What a rebuke for us! If this text, preached to a group of people by a preacher whose heart was on fire, could set in operation the modern missionary enterprise, what might we expect today if this call could be thrown into the hearts of our people? It has a definite challenge in it that needs to be sounded in our ears. God grant that we may hear God's call to our hearts to *lengthen cords and strengthen stakes* so that His blessings may be poured out.

Ho, every one that thirsts, come ye to the waters, . . . come ye, buy, eat. Wherefore do you spend money for that which is not bread? And your earnings for that which does not satisfy? (55:1, 2.)

This is the invitation that God gives to His people in the light of the salvation made possible by the Suffering Servant. With all the rich blessings of full pardon available He sends His prophet to proclaim a hearty invitation to all men everywhere. The questions he asks are arresting and thought-provoking. They still need to come to people who are spending their money for that which gives no abiding satisfaction. God is rich in grace and salvation and peace for every man who will call upon Him. Oh, that men would join in a world-wide heralding of this message until every soul has been able to answer these questions.

> *Seek ye the Lord while he may be found, call ye upon Him while he is near: let the wicked forsake his way, and the unrighteous man his thoughts; and let him return unto the Lord, and he will have mercy upon him; and to our God, for he will abundantly pardon.* (55:6, 7.)

You must forsake your sins. You must seek Him at the right time. You must seek Him with all your heart. You may be sure of realizing full restoration as He comes to bless you. Seek to know Him, to be reconciled with Him, to enjoy His pardoning grace. He may now be found. It will be too late one of these days. The choice is urgent. Jesus said: "I am the way, the truth and the life. No man cometh unto the Father but by me." Jeremiah represents God as saying: "Ye shall seek me and ye shall find me, when ye seek me with all your heart." How marvelous to be promised the blessings of eternal life!

> *It is your iniquities that separate between you and your God. And your sins make him hide His face from you, that He will not hear. For your hands are defiled with blood and your fingers with iniquity.*
> (59:2, 3.)

Sin is the one cause for heart loneliness and despair. Instead of self-pity, complaining and charges against God the sinner is reminded that he is responsible for all the misery and distress that he suffers. God has given the honor of free choice so that the responsibility is on him. When hands and fingers are defiled with behavior that is unbecoming, the individual may be certain of divine displeasure and punishment.

> *The Spirit of Yahweh is upon me, because He has anointed me to announce good tidings . . . to bind up . . . to proclaim liberty . . . to give to them a garland for ashes.* (61:1-3.)

The Servant learns that His mission is to announce the end of pain and suffering, to proclaim the era of God's favor, and to speak of God's vengeance. His ministry is to be evangelistic, healing, preaching, comforting, and joy-giving. When Jesus came to select the best picture of Himself, He turned to this portrait (Luke 4:17-22). He realized that He was called to go to the poor, the broken-hearted, the captives, the blind and the mourners.

> *Like one whom his mother comforts, so will I comfort you.* (66:13.)

When did you think of God as having the qualities of a mother? We are familiar with the idea of the fatherhood of God. Jesus came to make that doctrine clearer and more precious to us. In this passage we see God's grace displayed as a mother who tenderly comforts her child. It adds a bit to our doctrine of God and gives us a sense of the loving heart that beats for His own children.

PRACTICAL LESSONS OF PERMANENT VALUE

1. A vision of God always brings a consciousness of personal unworthiness.
2. The first impulse of a cleansed heart is to seek to lead others to Him.
3. A consciousness of His presence makes any task appear possible.
4. Ingratitude and rebellion break the heart of an affectionate father.

5. Blessing and obligation are inseparable. Privilege brings corresponding responsibility.

6. A life is never a failure when lived according to the will of God.

7. A great faith in God will give needed courage in the darkest hour of danger.

8. Genuine heart change is more important than conformity to rules of ritual.

9. If nations and individuals could let God settle disputes wars would cease.

10. When God calls a prophet He will provide the needed power for victory.

11. A man's conception of sin is built around and molded by his idea of God.

12. God's righteousness can be a devouring flame penetrating the world, burning wickedness as chaff or stubble.

13. Sin causes the sense of the soul to atrophy so that men lose the power of perceiving moral distinctions.

››› MICAH ‹‹‹

It is good to find a worthy champion of the poor who has courage and power to deliver an effective message. Knowing his fellows so intimately Micah was able to present in vivid colors the challenge to justice and consideration. His profound sympathy with the oppressed people came to life in unforgettable words. His spirit burned with righteous indignation as he saw the rank injustice practiced upon his neighbors and friends. The poor peasants of Judah had a strong champion in this powerful young preacher from the country.

The Background

Historical and political. The last half of the eighth century takes its place as the golden age of Old Testament prophecy. While Amos and Hosea preached in the North, Isaiah and Micah brought God's message to the people in the South. It was a period of turmoil, strife, change and growth. World problems were tackled and solutions found. Assyria coming rapidly to front rank as a world power, invaded and destroyed both Syria and Israel. The shadow of Assyria's armies was cast over Judah and the lowlands of Philistia.

In 745 B.C. Tiglath Pileser III began his reconquest of the West. The Aramean power with its allies in northern Syria was first broken. The year 738 B.C. saw the Assyrian armies in Damascus and at the gates of Samaria with Rezin and Menahem paying huge sums in tribute money. This invasion marked the beginning of the end for these two nations.

Depending upon Egypt for help the king of Syria (Rezin) and the king of Israel (Pekah) determined to unite the peoples of the West in a revolt from Assyria. They had grown tired of paying tribute to the Assyrians. Jotham of Judah could not be drawn into this foolish scheme, and his son and successor, Ahaz, was attacked by the two kings. Jerusalem was captured and sacked before help could come to Ahaz. It was a dark hour for Jerusalem. The weak Ahaz used the little gray matter that he had at his disposal and invited the great Tiglath Pileser to come up to save him. Nothing could please the Assyrian more than to comply with such a request. In short order he appeared in Rezin's realm with an army sufficient to break the Syrian power and overthrow the king. In the year 732 B.C. the city of Damascus and practically all the land of Israel fell before Tiglath Pileser's armies. Ahaz of Judah was forced to journey to Damascus to confirm his allegiance to Assyria and to accept his place as a puppet king under Assyrian control.

Thus the small kingdoms of the West were completely under the sway of Assyria before the death of Tiglath Pileser in 728 B.C. Samaria was left as a small city with a vassal king over it. Hoshea was content to pay the heavy tribute for a short time only. When he rebelled, the forces of Shalmanezer moved up against the heavily fortified city and began a siege that ended, after three years, in the capture and destruction of Omri's capital. Thus in 722 B.C. the eclipse of the Northern Kingdom was complete. Captivity had come for Jeroboam's kingdom after 209 years.

Sargon II became the new ruler of Assyria and continued until his death in 705 B.C. The land of Israel was practically depopulated with more than 27,000 captives taken away. Assyrian garrisons were introduced with governors to carry out the orders of the king of Assyria. Captives from many regions were brought in to fill up the land of Israel.

In 720 B.C. a new revolt in the West proved fruitless. Ahaz of Judah, remaining loyal to Assyria, refused to have a part in the uprising. But when Hezekiah came to the throne in Jerusalem he gradually turned from Assyria to lean on Egypt. In his reforms he threw out the Assyrian altar which Ahaz had brought back from Damascus in 732 B.C.

In 715 B.C. Ashdod led in another general revolt. Judah,

Edom and Moab, relying on Egypt, refused to send tribute to Sargon. In 711 B.C. Sargon came against the West with a powerful army, inflicting severe punishment upon the rebels. In some way Hezekiah and the people of Jerusalem escaped and the Holy City was spared. It was during these stormy days that Isaiah and Micah were preaching in Judah.

At the death of Sargon in 705 B.C. the powerful young Sennacherib came into power in Assyria. During his first three years he was kept busy trying to overcome Merodach Baladan of Babylonia and other rebels who seized the opportunity to rebel against the new king.

In the West, Shabaka of Egypt, Luli of Sidon, Hezekiah of Judah, and some of the smaller kingdoms had engineered a dangerous revolt against the new Assyrian monarch. Sennacherib with a large army left Nineveh in 701 B.C. to subdue the disturbers and administer a stinging rebuke to the Egyptian troublemakers.

Step by step the legions of Sennacherib moved on into the West. When Sidon was taken the kingdom of Phoenicia collapsed. Immediately Philistia was invaded by the victorious Assyrians. Shabaka of Egypt came to the rescue and a battle was fought at Eltekeh. Though the outcome is not fully known, the power of Egypt was severely shaken. Soon the cities of Philistia and the other towns of Palestine were at the mercy of Sennacherib. Of all the cities of the land only Jerusalem remained. Hezekiah and Isaiah, depending on Yahweh, kept the people from surrender. A great deliverance came when one hundred and eighty-five thousand soldiers were suddenly smitten. Yahweh came to the rescue of His chosen people. Sennacherib fled to his own land leaving Hezekiah and his people praising Yahweh, their great Saviour.

It was a stirring time with all sorts of changes and disturbances. Ahaz, Hezekiah, Rezin, Isaiah, Micah, Tiglath Pileser, Shalmanezer, Sargon, and Shabaka played their parts in the rapidly moving drama. God was leading His followers and gradually working out His own great purpose in the world.

Social conditions. The country preacher knew the tragic situation in Judah and Israel. Out where social wrongs are more keenly felt than anywhere else, he was able to sense the suffering of the peasants under the cruel pressure of men who had power. The judges were venal, the priests were immoral and corrupt, the prophets were hirelings, the nobles took peculiar delight in fleecing the poor, and the entire group had built up a wall of enmity, fear and hatred that made life miserable for all classes.

> *They covet fields, and seize them and houses, and take them away: and they oppress a man and his house. (2:2.)*
> *Haters of good and lovers of evil, tearing their skin from upon them and their flesh from their bones.*
> *(3:2.)*

The nation was ready for a collapse. The princes, the priests, the prophets and the people were responsible for its downfall.

> *Ye abhor justice, and twist all that is straight, building Zion with blood, and Jerusalem with iniquity. Her chiefs judge for a bribe, her priests teach for hire, her prophets divine for money; and yet they lean on the Lord, saying, Is not Yahweh in the midst of us? Evil cannot come on us. (3:9b-11.)*

Callous greed and cruelty mark the ungodly conduct of men who should behave humanely.

> *Ye strip the robe from off the garment from these who pass by unsuspectingly, averse to war. `The women of my people ye tear from their pleasant homes; from their children ye take away my glory forever. (2:8b-9.)*

The people were so greedy for wealth that no step was too low for them if a bit of money was involved. The Naboth vineyard experience was re-enacted on all sides. Certainly a prophet was sorely needed.

Religious conditions. On every hand there was a spirit utterly foreign to the sort of religious fervor that the prophet desired. A scornful, reckless type of irreligion was prevalent. The people did not want any preaching done except the weak, insipid variety that would allow them to go on in their way without embarrassment. It is a tragic hour when people will hear only the man who panders to their selfish, immoral nature.

> *If a man who walks in wind and falsehood should deceive thee, saying, I will preach to thee of wine and strong drink; he would be the preacher of this people.* (2:11.)

Soothsaying, witchcraft, superstition and idolatry were prevalent in the land. The Assyrian practices and cults were still influencing religious behavior. The people were lacking in integrity to such an extent that no one could be trusted.

> *The good man has perished from the land, and of the upright among men there is none: they all are lurking for blood; every man hunts his brother with a net. The best of them is like a thornbush, the most honest is like a thorn hedge. Trust not a friend, put not confidence in a familiar friend: a man's enemies are the men of his own house.* (7:2, 4, 5, 6b.)

The prophets and priests were corrupt, selfish, immoral and greedy. What good could come from such leadership? These men were guilty of the sort of behavior that kills spiritual glow. They merely wanted money, ease, cheap popularity and some assurance that they could continue to live in luxury. They were willing to make war on all those who opposed them.

> *Who lead my people astray; biting with their teeth they preach peace; and against him who gives them nothing for their mouths they consecrate war.* (3:5.)

The sins of the times have been summarized as follows: [1]

1. Oppression of the poor 2:2, 8, 9; 3:1-4.
2. Unscrupulous use of power 2:1f.; 3:10.
3. Lack of integrity 6:12; 7:2-6.
4. Reckless scorn of religion 3:5-8; 5:12-14.
5. False prophets 3:5, 7, 9-11.
6. Greedy corruption in church and state 7:3.

THE MAN

How many of us could identify Micah if he should meet us on the street? By careful study we may learn the man so thoroughly that he will walk before us, speak his message, rebuke the rulers and other prophets, weep with the sufferers, predict brighter days ahead, and interpret for us the will of God. In so doing we will be able to read, understand and interpret his book as would his own contemporaries.

His origin. Micah was a native of a small village near the Philistine border by the name of Moresheth-Gath. Jerusalem was only twenty miles away. Tekoa, the home of Amos, was only seventeen miles to the east. Ashdod, Gaza and Lachish were within the same radius. The great international highway from Assyria to Egypt ran through the valley in full view. Through this quiet village passed the messengers and diplomats from the court at Jerusalem enroute to Egypt. It was an ideal place for a young prophet to live and learn and preach. Micah was a country man who looked with distrust upon the residents of the cities, and yet he must have learned

[1] Cf. Merrill, *Prophets of the Dawn,* pp. 147-150. Used by permission of the publishers, Fleming H. Revell.

to love his capital city with a sincere devotion. He was keenly aware of world events and their significance. His lowly origin made him capable of seeing things in a light that might well be coveted by statesmen the world over.

His date. In the introductory statement we are told that Micah preached during the days of Jotham, Ahaz and Hezekiah. This would place his activity during the years between 738 B.C. and 698 B.C. According to Jer. 26:18 he was active in the days of Hezekiah. The opening prophecy in his book was certainly directed against Samaria before the siege and fall of that city in 722 B.C. It may be that he continued his ministry for a short while in the early reign of Manasseh. He was, at any rate, active during the last third of the eighth century. Isaiah and Hosea were his contemporaries. He probably knew Amos. The four prophets formed a mighty quartet in that troublous age.

His equipment. One finds himself strangely limited in trying to arrive at the full evaluation of Micah's equipment. How much did his own home contribute? What sort of father and mother taught him? How poor was he? Did Amos exert a real influence over him? Was he on friendly and intimate terms with the prophet Isaiah?

It would be great to find answers for these questions. At any rate it is good to be confronted with the questions. Surely the home, the parents, the neighbors, the circumstances made their separate contributions. Micah was most probably a peasant farmer who had a natural suspicion of the cities. Samaria and Jerusalem were the places where vice and wickedness and irreligion were concentrated. The wealthy nobles who fleeced the poor lived in these cities. The rulers, the princes, the judges, the priests, the false prophets were making their home in the cities. Something happened in the young heart of Micah that was to set him against oppression, vice, immorality, unscrupulous use of power, and shallow religious thinking. It was a valuable training.

George Adam Smith says: "The lowlands that held his

village are sufficiently detached from the capital and the body
of the land to beget in her sons an independence of mind and
feeling, but so much upon the edge of the open world as to
endue them at the same time with that sense of the responsibilities of warfare, which the national statesmen aloof and at
ease in Zion, could not possibly have shared." [2]

His real equipment however, was of a finer and more
valuable nature. He says:

> *But I truly am full of power by the Spirit of*
> *Yahweh, and justice and might, to declare to Jacob*
> *his transgression, and to Israel his sin.* (3:8.)

He had ethical integrity, courage and unflinching truth-
fulness in speaking the whole counsel of God to the nobles,
the judges, the rulers and the prophets. He was God's man,
with peculiar endowments and with enough courage to drive
relentlessly on in the doing of the divine will.

His personality. In his likes, his dislikes, his convictions
and his emphasis on social righteousness, Micah was definitely akin to Amos and Elijah. He was a true patriot who
loved his land, his capital city, but most of all his own poor,
downtrodden people. His convictions were rooted and
grounded so deeply that he was able to maintain a stern,
powerful, fearless front in denouncing the evils of his day.
His unfeigned sincerity carried weight wherever he went.
His passion for righteousness drove him forth with a flaming
word for those who lacked ethical standards. The "unsophis-
ticated rustic" was always seeking justice and mercy for his
peasant friends who suffered so bitterly. He was an artist in
using figures, similes, descriptions and words that carried
peculiar weight. Smith says: "While Micah spoke he had
wasted lives and bent backs before him—pinched, peasant
faces peer between all his words." [3]

Estimates of the man. Merrill says: "This man may have

[2] *Ibid.*, p. 377.
[3] *Ibid.*, p. 156.

been the least of the four. He may seem to plod his way
where the others mount up with wings as eagles. But to him
it was given through the inspiration of God to state as no
other has ever done the simple majestic unalterable essentials of true religion." [4]

Cohon says: "Micah had the peasant's suspicion of the
city, his strong, natural prejudice against luxury, self-indulgence, and vices of the city. Fearless, merciless, severe, he
denounced with the unflinching justice of Amos and, nevertheless, pleaded with the deep compassion of Hosea. The cry
of the poor woke prophecy in his soul." [5]

J. M. P. Smith says: "Knowing his fellow countrymen intimately, and sympathizing profoundly with their sufferings
and their wrongs, his spirit burned with indignation as he
beheld the injustice and tyranny of their rich oppressors." [6]

James says: "Micah proved just one more voice crying in
the name of Yahweh against 'man's inhumanity to man.' His
is a particularly poignant voice when he speaks of the wrongs
done to the poor. There is no denunciation in the Bible of
the oppressing rich more telling than the opening words of
his second chapter. And in the age-long struggle of Israel's
nobler minds to work out something of that equality between rich and poor which they believed was the will of
God Micah played a right manful part." [7]

Ward says: "Micah provides an interesting study. He belonged to the people; his sympathies were with those whose
life he shared. Far from the madding crowd of those contending for favor and preferment, he looked at things not
with the eye of a diplomatist or the party intriguer, but with
the clear vision of the onlooker who sees most of the game." [8]

Leslie says of 6:8: "Nothing in the Old Testament sur-
passes this statement as a summary of the prophetic view of

---

[4] *Ibid.*, p. 78.
[5] *Ibid.*, p. 78.
[6] *Ibid.*, p. 216.
[7] *Ibid.*, p. 281.
[8] *Ibid.*, p. 125.

the requirements Yahweh makes of his worshipers. The true religious genius of Israel throbs in these words. As J. M. P. Smith says, they link ethics with piety, bringing together in a mighty synthesis duty toward God and man." [9]

Gordon says: "Micah lacked his (Isaiah's) breadth of vision, but he saw deeper into the heart of things. In his eyes the Kingdom of God was based on no earthly citadel, however splendid or steadfast, but in the hearts of living men and women, the simple ones who feared God and did his will—a real foregleam of the truth which Jesus first made clear, that 'God is Spirit; and they that worship him must worship in spirit and in truth' (John 4:24)." [10]

Oesterley and Robinson say: "He differs from Amos, however, in being more deeply in sympathy with the sufferings of the oppressed peasantry; we are left with the impression that he was himself under the harrow. Micah had a fervid and vigorous personality, and employed powerful modes of expression. No prophet is more bitter—we might almost say more savage—in his condemnation of the social evils of his day. Like Amos, he stood for righteousness; and for a type of righteousness which gave full value to the rights and needs of human personality." [11]

Sellin says: "His exhortations to repentance addressed to the rich, the judges and the prophets are inspired by the deepest moral earnestness; he is in this respect an Amos redivivus." [12]

Huxley says of 6:8: "A perfect ideal of religion! A conception of religion which appears to me as wonderful an inspiration of genius as the art of Phidias or the science of Aristotle!"

[9] *Ibid.*, p. 198.
[10] *The Prophets of the Old Testament*, p. 140. Harper & Brothers.
[11] *An Introduction to the Books of the Old Testament*, p. 385. MacMillan & Company.
[12] *Introduction to the Old Testament*, p. 178. Harper & Brothers.

The Book

The book by Micah stands sixth among the prophets in the Hebrew Bible but is found in third place in the Septuagint. "Micah" is an abbreviated form of the longer name "Micaiah" and means "Who is like Yahweh?"

Contents and outline. We have a collection of the addresses and sermons of Micah arranged logically to carry forward the general scheme of corruption, punishment, correction, salvation of a small remnant and beautiful promises for the future blessedness of Zion. Samaria and Jerusalem are denounced as guilty before the great Judge of the universe. Captivity and exile are inevitable. Social injustice is rebuked. Unfaithfulness and dishonesty are denounced; heathenish abuses are combated and judgment on Samaria, Jerusalem and the Temple is positively announced. Certain deliverance from Babylon is promised, and a new city and nation are foretold. The Messianic pictures are exceptionally beautiful.

1, 2　The doom of Samaria and Jerusalem.
　　　A small remnant will be saved.
　　　　1:2-16　The two capitals must be destroyed.
　　　　2:1-11　Causes of the judgment.
　　　　2:12, 13　A promise of restoration.
3:1-5:15　The sins of the prophets and the leaders. This present devastation to give way to exaltation.
　　　　3:1-12　The rulers and prophets are corrupt and godless.
　　　　4:1-5:15　A messianic picture of restoration and glory.
6, 7　Yahweh's great controversy with Israel and its ultimate outcome. The claims of genuine religion. The way of salvation given.

Some predictions. In the book we find the following definite predictions:

1. Samaria, the capital of Israel, to fall   1:6, 7.
2. Jerusalem and its Temple to be destroyed   3:12; 7:13.
3. The people of Judah to be taken to Babylon   4:10.
4. God's people to be brought back from captivity   4:1-8;
   7:11, 14-17.
5. The Messiah to be born in Bethlehem   4:8; 5:2-4.
6. Universal peace to come when men of all nations learn
   at His feet   4:1-5.

Style of the Book. Micah used a vigorous, vivid, fresh,
straightforward style that pictured clearly the tragic situation
about him. He loved to follow the law of recurrence, using
the same material over and over with added details here and
there. Many of his sentences are involved and seemingly disconnected. Flashes of indignation, vivid descriptions, beautiful promises, follow one another in rapid succession. He was
fond of historical references and, while bringing them in, he
indulged frequently in dramatic interruptions and answers.
He used good, terse, classic Hebrew. The lyrical passages
easily took the form of a prayer or a psalm. For a modern
reader who knows little of Palestine and the actual happenings of Micah's day the book appears confused, difficult and
practically meaningless.

Integrity of the book. Until the middle of the nineteenth
century there was little question concerning the unity of the
book. Micah was thought to be the author of all of it. He
lived, preached and wrote during the days of Jotham, Ahaz
and Hezekiah of Judah. The tendency of modern critical
scholarship, however, is to say that the eighth century prophet
wrote the first three chapters, and that the other chapters
were composed by later authors. James would classify the
following passages as late: 2:12, 13; 4:1-5:9; and 7:7-20.
Eiselen, after a long and careful weighing of all the evidence
is inclined to accept all of the book except 7:7-20 as the work
of Micah. He thinks these verses are definitely late.

Dr. J. L. Green, after an exhaustive study of language,

style, historical standpoints and logical inferences, says: "External evidence clearly points to Mican authorship of the entire book. In places, internal evidence argues for unity; in other sections it is neutral; in a few passages it points toward composite authorship. Until more conclusive proof in the direction of composite authorship is presented, however, the writer accepts the book as a unity. At the same time he recognizes that the arguments against the authenticity of chapters 6, 7 and of chapter 7:7-20 especially, have considerable weight. The book is certainly not the patchwork of interpolations that it is sometimes said to be. It is a great book with a timeless message, coming largely, if not altogether, from the eventful ministry of a powerful peasant preacher, Micah, the Morashtite." [13]

The issue will always remain unsettled. There is very little convincing evidence that would drive us to accept a late date for any part of the book. Certainly we are not forced to give up the great majority of chapters four to seven. For our purpose we are dealing with all sections of the book as the word of God to us.

His idea of God. Micah sought to socialize and ethicize the current, popular conception of God. The people of his day were very religious but they needed a richer and a more humanized religion. Micah wanted the people to know that every unsocial act was an insult to God. In His own way God looks on the conduct of rulers and nobles who drive the poor from their homes, plunder the public, steal, bribe and pander to the wealthy, and He is deeply offended by their behavior. Because of all these offenses the Lord is determined to bring them into judgment. For Yahweh is a God, glorious in power, holy in character and aim, careful to make definite demands on His people.

He is a Judge 1:3, 6; 3:12. Because of unrighteous conduct the people must suffer unbelievable consequences.

[13] Thesis, *The Problem of Unity in Micah.*

He is a God of ethical righteousness 6:8; 2:1, 2; 3:2, 3, 10, 11; 7:2.

He is a God who converts the world through Zion 5:7; 4:2.

He is a God who loves peace 4:3; 5:5.

He is a God of hope and promise 7:7, 18-20.

Preaching Values

The book has a distinct message for our day. The same righteous God who has never lowered His high ethical standards, is working out the same great purpose and is anxious to lead us to exhibit the same high, moral conduct that Micah urged upon his people. The challenge of the words of this country preacher is tremendous. Let him come to our congregations today to break us with this fresh message. Religion to him meant fair dealing, restraint, downright honesty, consideration, integrity, and a close walk with a friendly God.

Some great texts

> *Hear, all ye people,*
> *Hearken, O earth, and its fullness;*
> *Let the Lord Yahweh be witness among you.* (1:2.)

The prophet pictures Yahweh as thoroughly aroused over the serious situation in the land. God is not asleep. He is alert, active, anxious about His people. Giant wrongs and rank injustices must be dealt with by a visitation from His holy Temple. God sits in judgment upon people who have caused so much grief and agony among their fellow men.

> *Woe to those who devise mischief*
> *And work out evil on their beds*
> *When the morning is light they put it into execution*
> *Because it is in the power of their hand.* (2:1-11.)

The sins of the people are put before us in blunt frankness. They are accused of the prostitution of high privilege. Selfish men lie awake working out pernicious plans to plunder poor, defenseless peasants. Covetousness leads to land-grabbing, eviction and slavery. This unscrupulous use of power is an inexcusable crime. Responsibility, wealth, position and prestige should humble them and cause them to dedicate themselves to a high task. Instead, greed attempts to silence the reformer who demands righteous conduct. These sinners are coarsened and degraded until sacred things and institutions are despised. They acquire a low conception of the preacher and his preaching. Only exile can remedy the situation. Therefore God will bring cruel suffering upon them.

> *I will surely gather thee, O Jacob, in mass;*
> *I will surely bring together the remnant of Israel. . . .*
> *Their king is passed on before them with Yahweh*
> *at their head.* (2:12f.)

The prophet has a message of hope for the exiles. Yahweh is a merciful God who bestows undeserved favor upon the repentant people. The gathering home will be certain, tender and gracious. The people will be safe and protected under the guidance of the Shepherd. *Yahweh is at their head* (cf. Psalm 23).

> *Haters of good and lovers of evil,*
> *Tearing their skin from upon them,*
> *And their flesh from their bones;*
> *Who eat the flesh of my people . . .*
> *Who abhor justice and distort all that is straight,*
> *Building Zion with bloodshed and Jerusalem with*
> *   iniquity.*
> *Her chiefs judge for a bribe,*
> *Her priests teach for hire,*

Her prophets divine for money:
Yet they lean on Yahweh, saying,
Is not Yahweh in our midst?
Evil cannot come upon us. (3:1-3, 9-11.)

Judges, priests, prophets and rulers are represented as cannibals at a great feast, devouring the poor, defenseless people. Cruelty, crookedness, corruption and oppression must be severely punished by a righteous God who cannot continue to look upon such inhuman behavior. Their cries for mercy will go unanswered in the day of their calamity. It is a serious crime to *lead people astray* and *consecrate a war against him who gives no bribe.* These timeservers will be left helpless when God turns his back upon them. *The sun will go down on the prophets.*

But I am full of power by the Spirit of Yahweh, and
justice, and might,
To declare to Jacob his transgression, and to Israel
his sin. (3:8.)

The true prophet is revealed as he stands forth in holy boldness. In contrast to the mercenary timeservers Micah claims a fresh courage, born of the indwelling Spirit. His power is set for a positive, passionate protest against the wrongs of his day. What a powerful preacher he was! God used him in burning his message into selfish hearts.

In latter days the mountain of Yahweh's house will
be established on the head of the mountains,
And it will be exalted above the hills
And peoples will flow to it.
Many nations will go and say,
Come, let us go up to the mountain of Yahweh. . . .
That he may instruct us from his ways,
And that we may walk in his paths;
And he will judge between many peoples,
And give decisions to strong nations. (4:1-3.)

This quotation has been described as "set like an oasis in the midst of desolations of wickedness and injustices, or like a towering mountain peak rising in lonely grandeur above the miasmic swamps of selfish materialism." It is truly the vision splendid. These promises should come to drooping hearts as a tonic to restore vigor, hope, stability and faith.

In an hour when billions are being poured out to provide death-dealing implements of war it is good to see God's ageless vision of a people sitting together about the eternal Arbiter. Disputes, differences, wars, hatreds and misunderstandings will be out of the question when He teaches, judges, and directs our lives. He will be able to bring about a condition of mind that will make universal peace possible. War colleges, war paraphernalia and war ideas will give place to peaceful pursuits. In His own good time we shall see the fulfillment of this divine vision for His creatures.

> *Every man shall sit under his vine*
> *And under his fig tree;*
> *With none to make them afraid*
> *For the mouth of the Lord has spoken it.* (4:4.)

The prophet has given us a glimpse into an ideal home where security, contentment, tranquillity and genuine happiness reign. He realizes that domestic tranquillity is the basis for international good will and equity among the peoples of the earth. When the home is happy and secure we may expect things to move on an even keel. Spiritual forces must be cultivated and released before this can be true. The spiritual must make the home secure. The chaotic conditions of the world grow out of the chaos of domestic life. Micah believed that the people who came and sat at the feet of the Messiah would be changed and fortified so that the homes of the land would be transformed. It is a challenge to us to get right with God and then seek to make our homes fit places for His presence.

Be in pain, and writhe, O daughter of Zion
For now must thou go forth from the city
And dwell in the field, and come to Babylon.
There Yahweh will redeem thee. (4:10.)

Before the end of the eighth century God gave, through his prophet, the program for Judah. It included (1) anguish, (2) suffering, (3) punishment, (4) exile, (5) return, (6) a new kingdom of redeemed souls, and (7) the evangelization of the nations through the work of this holy remnant. Babylon will hold them for a season but Jerusalem is to live again so that the peoples of the earth may hear the good news. The purpose of God will be realized in spite of sin, captivity and suffering. God is never in a hurry. We may grow impatient and complain but He moves triumphantly on in His victorious march toward the hour when all men shall come to Him in humility and devoted surrender.

But thou, Bethlehem Ephrathah, smallest among
the thousands of Judah,
Out of thee will come forth to me One who is to be
ruler in Israel.
He will stand and will shepherd in the strength of
Yahweh
And this One shall be our peace. (5:2-5a.)

Little Bethlehem is to be signally honored in the coming of the Anointed One who *will stand and feed* his flock, gather the residue of his brethren, establish them by divine power and universal influence, protect them from the nations, make them a supernatural influence among many peoples, remove the love of militarism and idolatry from them, and establish His name among them forever.

This picture of a divine Conqueror is to find its fulfillment in the Christ who won His victories not by might, or by power, but by His Spirit. He came as a lowly babe from remote Bethlehem to bring salvation to a world so sorely in need of a Saviour. When the Wise Men came to Jerusalem seeking the new King they were guided to Bethlehem by this seven hundred year old word from Micah (cf. Matt. 2:6; John 7:42). To that little city came the highest event and the holiest personality in all Israel's history.

> *And the remnant of Jacob will be in the midst of*
> *   many peoples*
> *Like dew from the Lord, Yahweh,*
> *Like showers upon the grass.* (5:7.)

We are indebted to Micah for the figure of the refreshing qualities of God's remnant. *Dew from Yahweh, showers upon the grass,* are God's gifts to a world that needs the vitalizing, creative, refreshing touch of the divine Giver. The prophet sees the sway of the remnant and the lift of the chosen few. The Master's minority composed of a few rare souls has ever been God's instrument in molding a finer social order. Such a remnant is always powerful, in many instances creative. God can do wonders through the group that is willing to separate itself in genuine consecration to the will of the Master.

> *He hath shewed thee, O man, what is good,*
> *And what doth Yahweh require of thee:*
> *But to do justly, to love mercy,*
> *And to walk humbly with thy God?* (6:8.)

In a dramatic paragraph Micah presents Yahweh in a lawsuit with His people. It is a solemn moment when their God enters into a controversy with them to set forth genuine religion and its claims. Impressively He reminds them of the many things He has done for them through the years. Mercy and goodness have been showered upon them in profusion. When their hearts are ready to break under the weight of God's tender kindness to them they inquire concerning God's demands upon them.

Micah presents the simple essentials of real religion in a

verse that has taken its place among the truly great Scripture treasures. Israel can hope for life only in an honest judiciary, good business ethics, a sincere group of prophets, a devoted priesthood, a considerate nobility, and a people who walk humbly with God. Micah begs them to exhibit true ritual, true worship, true morality, that will eventuate in true behavior. He does not substitute morality for religion. Outward conduct is essential but it always depends on inward character. That inward character in turn depends on personal communion with God. Sellin says that this forms "one of the most imposing passages of the Old Testament before the spirit of which all other oriental religions hide their downcast heads." [14]

The chief notes of this genuine religion are reality, ethical soundness, distrust of form and ritual, righteous conduct and the primacy of personal experience. Religion must work itself out in right social institutions and translate mercy into daily deeds by a close, personal walk with a loving God. Yahweh demands their life, their love, their trust, their loyalty. Eiselen says: "Yahweh's good will is secured not by carefully observing the ritual, but by living in harmony with the principles of righteousness, by diligently practicing kindness and brotherliness, and by maintaining a living fellowship with God in the spirit of humility." [15]

Over against the elaborate sacrificial system practiced by the Israelites Micah puts this clear, brief, comprehensive statement of the essence of true worship. Merrill says: "He gathers up into a single sentence the gist of the messages of the other three prophets. The keynote of Amos' teaching is *justice*. Hosea strikes the richer, deeper note of *love*. Isaiah calls for reverent, *humble fellowship* with the Holy One. These are their characteristic messages. The 'Religion of the Spirit' has dawned. It is still a long way to the fulness of

[14] *Ibid.*, p. 178.
[15] *Ibid.*, p. 491.

noon; but the true light is shining, and shall shine more and more unto the perfect day in Christ Jesus." [16]

PRACTICAL LESSONS OF PERMANENT VALUE

1. Elaborate pretensions of piety and liberal gifts in public cannot atone for a lack of true righteousness in the heart. Religion and ethics are inseparable.
2. The unscrupulous use of power, even though within the bounds of law, hurts the heart of God.
3. Religion is a matter of the inner heart and makes the individual behave according to the leading of God.
4. We cannot expect God to continue rich blessings upon us when we are not in harmony with Him and His purpose for us.
5. Courage comes to a minister who senses the presence of God in his life.
6. The difference between the false prophet and the true prophet is not so much in creed as in conduct.
7. Universal peace will be assured when the peoples of the earth sit at the Messiah's feet and let Him arbitrate their disputes and guide their behavior.
8. The tragic state of a people whose leaders are unworthy.
9. The certainty of the triumph of God's purpose and His undertakings.
10. How reasonable are God's basic requirements! How unchangeable are His demands! How deep and tender and changeless His great love!

[16] *Ibid.,* p. 156.

··· JEREMIAH ···

No more colorful figure emerges from the pages of the Old Testament than the prophet Jeremiah. For a half century he lived and labored to attract men to the way of God. Tragically he stood in the main stream of rushing humanity warning the heedless throng of the certain destruction awaiting them. Madly they rushed on into death and exile over the struggling form of the faithful messenger of God. In all of these trying hours God sustained and strengthened His prophet.

His Times

No estimate of Jeremiah is complete without a glance at the reign and influence of Manasseh. He began his long career in 698 B.C. on the death of the good king Hezekiah. For fifty-five years he had control of the affairs of Judah. Esarhaddon (681-668 B.C.) and Assurbanipal (668-626 B.C.) exerted a powerful influence over him. He was forced to acknowledge the religion of the empire and to put down any local prophet or teacher who opposed such tendencies. Isaiah was probably executed by Manasseh's order. Much innocent blood was shed. The customs and habits of Assyria were brought in along with the religious practices. It was a dark day for Yahweh religion in the land of Judah.

Josiah came to the throne of Judah in 641 B.C. (or in 637 B.C.) with the terrific responsibility of changing the entire trend and turning a nation back to God. He was growing into young manhood during the closing days of Assurbanipal. Nabopolassar took over the reins of government in 626 B.C. and sounded the death knell for Assyria. The kingdom continued for several years until the fall of Nineveh in 612 B.C. but the new mistress was in the saddle as world ruler.

The cruel Scythians from the regions above the Black Sea

came through the land of Palestine with devastating effect
from 628-624 B.C. and continued their destructive work until
the final collapse of Nineveh. These savage hordes did much
to change the complexion of the world and to stir up Jeremiah and Zephaniah to preach.

In 623 B.C. Josiah started a thorough cleanup of the Temple and the religious life of the people. A strong impetus was
given the work when the Book of the Law was found in the
Temple. Vigorous efforts at reform resulted in revolutionary
changes in the religious situation. Perhaps Zephaniah had a
definite part in the reformation. We may be sure that Jeremiah was ardently interested in the religious reforms.

In 612 B.C. the grand old city of Nineveh fell under the
combined forces of the Medes, the Babylonians and the
Scythians. It was a tragic hour for the mighty kingdom. (Read
Nahum's account of the fall.) Babylon rapidly took her place
as the head of the world empire. The untimely death of
Josiah ruined any hope for the kingdom of Judah. Jerusalem
was to continue for more than twenty years but no ruler was
available who could lead in God's paths. Judah's sun was
gradually sinking. Exile was certain.

In 605 B.C. Nebuchadrezzar became king of Babylon and
Jehoiakim was placed on the throne of Judah. The Egyptians
were defeated at Carchemish thus closing the door forever
for Egypt. This Waterloo battle changed the history of the
world. Jehoiakim was a proud, godless, sinful creature who
was a constant thorn in the side of Jeremiah. The good work
of Josiah was largely lost as Jehoiakim took his stand against
the Yahweh religion.

In 598 B.C. Nebuchadrezzar was forced to come against
Jerusalem because of Jehoiakim's disloyalty. Jehoiachin was
placed on the throne for three months but his reign ended
disastrously when the city was captured and the best of the
citizens were taken along with the royal family to Babylon.
The wealth, the sacred vessels and the captives were transported to the land of Exile.

Zedekiah was left to rule in Jerusalem under the close supervision of Babylon. Daniel and Ezekiel were in Babylon. Jeremiah and Habakkuk were in Jerusalem. Only a few years were left for the inhabitants of Judah. A strong Egyptian party continued their insistence on a revolt, promising help from Pharaoh Hophra. Babylon was ready to destroy Jerusalem on the slightest provocation.

In 587 B.C. the Babylonians came to put an end to the rebellious nation. Jeremiah counseled immediate surrender and loyal obedience to Nebuchadrezzar's will as the only way for Judah to continue. Hophra came to the rescue of his neighbor but it was only a ripple on the surface, for nothing could stop the Babylonians. The relief was only temporary. The siege was continued. Famine, pestilence, hunger, despair and disease did their work along with the pounding of the army. The end came when a hole was made in the walls, the king's household fled and the city surrendered. Houses were burned, the walls were thrown down, the Temple was utterly destroyed and the people were dragged along in chains to Babylon.

Gedaliah was left as a representative of the Babylonian government to look after the people who remained in Judah. Jeremiah chose to stay with these same people although he could have gone to Babylon as a guest of the royal house. When Gedaliah was murdered the fear-stricken Jews took the old prophet with them to Egypt where he passed his latter days.

The *social conditions* faced by Jeremiah during his long career called for a wise head and courageous action. On every side he saw problems of class and family and foreign cults with their attendant miseries. The rich were powerful, unscrupulous, oblivious to the real needs of the poor, and interested only in that which would bring gain to themselves. The poor were driven to toil as slaves with almost no advantages for improvement of any kind. Discontent, hatred and envy filled their minds as they endured the misery of the passing days. Family life was deplorable. Slavery was common as early as 600 B.C. Robbery, murder, lying, and emphasis on a selfish hunt for material things, characterized the life of the people.

The *religious conditions* were not more pleasing. Jeremiah found a strange mixture of Canaan's nature religion, Jezebel's Baalism, Babylonian cults, and a natural tendency to an utterly meaningless formalism. Religious syncretism had done its worst and the merger was far from satisfactory. To the sensitive soul of Jeremiah the people were as bad as the heathen inhabitants of Canaan. He indicts them for un reality, sensualism, double-mindedness and outright degen eracy.

Josiah's reforms in 623-621 B.C. attempted the elimination of the superstitious practices, the suppression of the heathen sanctuaries and the purification of the Temple and its worship. Much good was accomplished but the movement failed to bring about the sort of revival of religion that the nation so sorely needed. Jeremiah realized how superficial and weak it was and how incapable the people were of understanding the basis for genuine spiritual religion. It was impossible to lift the people, the priests, and the other prophets, into the clear atmosphere of spiritual religion. They could not understand his language.

THE MAN

Jeremiah's *early training* in the priestly village of Anathoth had much to do with his personality and his career. Abiathar, David's great priest, established the village and his descendants continued to live in that quiet suburb of the Holy City. The young lad was brought up in the quiet company of scholars, priests, prophets and students of God's teachings. The effect of the changing world affairs, with the great crisis in Asia must have made a profound impression on the growing boy. The coming of the boy king, Josiah, to the throne was a momentous change in the life of the nation. It is conceivable that Jeremiah and Josiah were friends from earliest boyhood days. The coming of the bloodthirsty Scythians on their cruel raids brought fear and dread to the young heart.

The call to prophetic service made a profound impression on the boy from Anathoth. Suddenly he realized that God had been counting on him for a big task from the very moment of his birth. No man ever gets away from such a discovery. He was weak, timid and shy but he was prepared to hear God's voice. He was listening when the divine voice came to him. He was already well acquainted with world problems and understood how difficult it would be to get men to respond to a spiritual challenge. His reverence in the presence of Yahweh is exceptionally commendable. God said to him: *I knew thee, I formed thee, I sanctified thee, I appointed thee.* God takes the full responsibility for the choice, the career and the victory that is to attend his efforts. He continues by assuring the lad with such statements as: *I shall send thee, I shall command thee, I am with thee.* In addition to this golden assurance He gives him two encouraging illustrations to guarantee that God is presiding over the tumult in the world and that everything is under His control. The young man was overwhelmed with the terrific responsibility that rested upon him but he started out upon his mission with the certainty that he was God's chosen representative for a specific task. He knew that Yahweh would give power and wisdom for the victory.

His character is clearly pictured for us in the book that is open before us. His timid, sensitive, emotional, tender nature made him particularly capable of identifying himself with the miseries, the mistakes and the needs of others. In no sense was he a weak sentimentalist or a weeping prophet. Misunderstood by his own family, opposed by priest and prophet, shunned by his people, his life was a tragic experience. Even though he complained and questioned God's treatment of him he continued to urge his fellow citizens to turn to God for cleansing and deliverance.

He belonged to the upper class and had the respect of the aristocratic princes. The fact that he was able to employ an amanuensis and buy real estate would indicate that he was a man of substance. It is clear that he was a man of education and culture, being thoroughly acquainted with history, political life, literature, Egyptian cults and practices and the deeper things of God's revelation. His well-stocked and well-disciplined mind was capable of grasping and interpreting varying trends of thought and reasoning.

He was strangely bound by the divine compulsion that continually drove him into the midst of the people with God's message. He could not get away from the feeling that the hand of God had been laid on him, even before his entrance into the world. He was a child of destiny! No difficult situation could snatch the challenge of this realization from his mind. Eternity alone can reveal the effect of this consciousness.

He was a thoroughgoing rebel. Amos and Elijah had blazed the trail before him. The sensitive soul of the "rebel prophet" was severely shocked by the vulgar religion with its hollow mockery, its shallow stupidity and its worldly materialism. He burst forth in spontaneous revolt. Laughing at their silly gods he used scathing satire to indicate his utter abhorrence. Jehoiakim and his program of godless waste came in for a terrific attack. Kings, princes, diplomats and false prophets were blasted by his sharp tongue. In the hour of battle he opposed resistance and counseled surrender to the Babylonians. It was called "treason" and he was soundly hated as one who weakened the morale of the defenders of the city. Thus in the political, the social and the religious realm he was a dangerous rebel. In it all he was far ahead of his generation in insight, in daring statement and in genuine loyalty to his dearest Friend. He was in possession of spiritual truths that were to be given a fuller interpretation by the master Teacher.

As a statesman with a "world mind" he revealed the effect

of the Spirit upon an alert mind that is able to reveal un-
dreamed of wisdom. His commission was world-wide. His
penetrating mind looked beyond the momentary suffering of
the exile to the new world "cleansed, purged, released and
prepared" by the will of God. What a wise leader he could
have been if only they had listened to him!

Throughout his life he was continually conscious of the
hand of God upon his very person. This divine compulsion
doomed him to perpetual loneliness and to an unending opposition. As Yahweh's spokesman he was constantly going
counter to every current of his day. Eternity alone will reveal
the suffering, the heartaches, the loneliness and the distress
of soul that wrung the heart of God's loyal prophet. Disaster,
failure, hostility and certain captivity loomed as inevitable
rewards for his work. God continually wrestled with him to
make him strong; although confused and baffled and perplexed, the consciousness that his eternal Friend led the way
made him strong to carry on. He is characterized by simplicity, sensitiveness and strength. Thank God for such a
prophet.

Farley says: "A more crushing burden was never laid upon
mortal man. In the whole history of the Jewish race there has
been no such example of intense sincerity, unrelieved suffering, fearless proclamation of God's message, and unwearying
intercession of a prophet for his people as is found in the life
of Jeremiah. But the tragedy of his life is this, that he
preached to deaf ears and reaped only hate in return for his
love to his fellow-countrymen. He was lightly esteemed in
life, and he sank into the grave a broken-hearted man. From
being of no account as a prophet he came to be regarded as
the greatest of them all." [1]

Jeremiah's *religion* was an affair of his own inner heart.
Personal religion came into its own in the experiences of this
man of God. His loneliness forced him back on God and gave
him a vital consciousness of individual dependence upon the

[1] *Ibid.*, p. 174.

eternal One. As he fell back into the arms of a loving God he found the source of strength that carried him along through all the trying hours of his troublous career. He thus became the most spiritual of all the prophets. His hope for the ultimate triumph of God's purpose in His chosen people is especially remarkable when we realize that there was no hope of personal immortality in his religion. He had a more spiritualized conception of sin than the other prophets. Relentlessly he traced sin to its roots and found that the source of all sin lies in the individual heart. In reality sin is a spiritual disease springing from an inward infection and culminating in a serious malady. The cure lies in the individual heart and the probe must go deep in order to bring about the needed restoration. The evil will must give place to a good will. The divine Surgeon must do His work. Jeremiah represents God as having a continual pain in His heart because of intense love for His people. The culminating idea in Jeremiah's religion is his conception of the new covenant which God is to make with His favored ones.

Jeremiah and Jesus.[2] One hesitates to speak of any human being as resembling Jesus. It will not be out of place, however, to point out certain resemblances in the environment, the methods, the outlook, and the ministry of these two individuals.

1. They lived under similar world conditions. Babylon was on the point of destroying Jerusalem in Jeremiah's day while Rome was exercising rigid control when Jesus came. In both instances formalism had a strangle hold on religion.

2. Both Jeremiah and Jesus grew up in quiet country places where plenty of time was available for meditation.

3. Each of them came early to be rejected in the home community and by the other members of the family circle.

4. Neither of them had the joys and blessings of married life to help when priest and prophet and people opposed them.

[2] Cf. Gordon, *The Rebel Prophet*, p. 227. Harper & Brothers.

5. Each of them was painfully conscious of God's hand upon him in the early days of his life.

6. Both understood, despised and condemned the priests (scribes and Pharisees) as being blind leaders and false teachers.

7. Their methods of teaching were similar. The simplest child could understand and be blessed by their words.

8. Their conceptions of religion were almost identical. To them it was a thing of the heart. Formalism was despised.

9. Their attitudes toward the Temple and ritual and the sacrificial system were so nearly the same that we marvel at the similarity.

10. Both of them gave evidence of intimate fellowship with the Father. What a rich experience each of them had!

11. They had tender, yearning hearts that spent much time in weeping over the sinning people about them.

12. In the end of life each was considered a failure but in later days each has taken his place among the victors. Jeremiah died in Egypt after a long life of suffering. Jesus suffered in shame and disgrace to make the sacrifice that has brought salvation to countless millions.

THE BOOK

There is a wide variety of material in the book of Jeremiah. Baruch, his friend and secretary, was largely responsible for the collection and preservation of the different groups of material. One could wish for a more systematic arrangement of the various prophecies and memoirs so that a logical study could be made. We know from the account in chapter thirty-six that a second edition of the prophetical messages was produced after the destruction by Jehoiakim. Much of the biographical narrative was contributed by Baruch who spent his entire life in the company of the great prophet.

It is interesting to know that the LXX edition of Jeremiah differs from the Hebrew Masoretic text. Each of them is an independent witness in determining the true text. The Greek copy is 2700 words shorter than the Hebrew and differs in many particulars. Whole verses are omitted in chapters 10, 17, 33, 39, 48 and 51. In chapters 27 and 28 the LXX reproduces the material in abridged form while chapters 46-51 are transposed and put into the text after 25:13. The LXX has 100 words not found in the Hebrew text.

There are three definite parts:

1. Prophecies concerning Jerusalem and Judah, 2-35.
2. Biographical narratives, 36-45.
3. Prophecies concerning foreign nations, 46-51.

Chapter one gives an account of the call of the prophet and chapter 52 is a concluding word concerning Zedekiah.

PREACHING VALUES

The book of Jeremiah presents rich material for preaching. The expositor finds timely themes, suggestive texts and challenging calls to spiritual quickening. His treatment of sin and salvation will repay an exhaustive study. To him sin was the stubbornness of the evil heart as the root and ground of individual sins. Ingratitude and disloyalty to God are the most excruciating manifestations of sin. His doctrine of salvation corresponds with his deeper conception of sin. Instead of mere deliverance from poverty or peril or pain Jeremiah defines salvation as deliverance from sin itself with all its habits, desires and dispositions. The only remedy is found in God's miraculous response to the humble cry of a penitent sinner. He announces God's willingness to grant full forgiveness of sin to all who come to Him.

Farley says: "The *distinctively new elements* in the teaching of Jeremiah are these: First, he definitely separated religion from external helps, and established it on a purely spiritual basis. And secondly, since a spiritual religion can no longer be a merely national religion, Jeremiah transformed religion into a universal thing, the birthright of all mankind. A man needs only to be a man to have immediate and direct personal fellowship with God. Herein lies our great hope for the heathen world, and our warrant for missionary enterprise." [3]

SOME GREAT TEXTS

I knew thee . . . formed thee . . . consecrated thee . . . appointed thee . . . have put my words in thy mouth . . . will be with thee . . . have set thee to root out, pull down, destroy, overthrow, build, plant.
(1:5-10.)

These words came into the ear of a young man of Ana-thoth who was in tune with God and who understood something of God's right to demand absolute obedience. He was well acquainted with the world in which he lived and recognized the difficulty of the task.

God revealed to him the fact of his choice and sanctification for this great work. Such a solemn announcement must have stunned the young priest. What a responsibility! What rich promises! What a golden privilege! What a high honor! We do not wonder that his response was but a feeble cry indicating his weakness, his inadequacy for such a burden. God's encouraging assurances brought added solemnity to the hour, for it was now certain that the load was already laid on the trembling shoulders. *I have put my word in thy mouth.* Even though the tongue be weak, the body frail and the mind worried by fears, the results are assured, for God said, *I am with thee.* It was the beginning of a long career as a mighty prophet of God.

Therefore, gird up, arise, speak, be not dismayed. For I have made thee a fortified city, an iron pillar, a bronze wall. I am with thee to deliver thee. (1:17-19.)

After the dramatic call and the golden assurances the youthful Jeremiah was given two heartening illustrations of

[3] *Ibid.,* p. 170.

God's power and readiness to carry out His purpose. The
almond tree taught him that God was awake, alert and working at the task of carrying out His purpose. The boiling
caldron assured him that in the midst of terrible dangers
from the North God was presiding over the tumult and that
no harm could come to His chosen people except as He
chose to bring it.

Therefore. Since God is awake and active and since He is
actually presiding over the world, the stirring challenge is
thrown down to him. *Therefore gird up thy loins, arise,
speak.* The prophet cannot refuse one who is awake, sufficient, has a right to command, has a purpose for the world,
is presiding over every phase of life, and who promises to be
with him. He now dares go in the divine strength.

> *I remember the devotion of thy youth, the love of
> thine espousals, when thou didst follow me in the
> wilderness. Israel was consecrated to Yahweh. I
> brought you into the garden-land, but when ye
> went in, you defiled my land. (2:2, 3, 7.)*

The honeymoon is over. God reminds rebellious Israel of
the fervor and the warmth and the purity of the love streams
in the early days. She was desperately in love with her Lover
and the tender love made life full of music and joy and hope.
She was pure and clean and holy. No disloyalty or unclean
thought marred the beauty of her devotion. But now the
picture is heart-rending. God's heart is crushed with grief
and disappointment. Israel now is living in open sin. She
is unfaithful to the covenant vows. Other gods have stolen
her affection. She has ceased to love Yahweh and her conduct
is shameful in the extreme. In spite of all the precious gifts
bestowed upon her the faithless wife has despised the hand
that blessed her and plunged headlong in unspeakable
shame.

> *My people have changed their glory for what is*
> *profitless. My people have committed two evils: Me,*
> *the fountain of living waters they have forsaken, to*
> *hew out for themselves cisterns, cracked cisterns,*
> *that can hold no water.* (2:11, 13.)

Yahweh still claims these sinful people even though they have gone out after other lovers and broken His heart. His challenge to them is to read history, inquire among the unusual happenings of the earth, and take a trip to check on all the neighbors to see if anything like this has ever happened before. He has not broken a covenant, practiced any deceit or disregarded a promise, and yet Israel is guilty of this shameful infidelity. Idolaters are always faithful to their idols.

Jeremiah pictures the scene of a gushing fountain of sparkling, life-giving water, open to all, and satisfying the deepest need. Instead of enjoying the rich blessings of this spring the people of Israel have turned away to dig for themselves cisterns in the dry desert area. After frantic efforts and intense suffering they watch the rain from heaven fill the cisterns. In horror they realize that these man-made holes are utterly worthless and that the water runs rapidly away. What a tragedy that men who have access to fresh, cool, satisfying streams of living water should turn away to try for satisfaction in such a useless search! God is the source of life. He is sufficient for every need forever. He satisfies completely the thirst of man. Augustine said: "The soul was made for God and will never rest in peace till it rests in Him."

> *Where are thy gods that thou hast made for thy-*
> *self? Let them arise, if they can help thee in the day*
> *of thy calamity.* (2:28.)

An arresting question is thus directed at people who fancy themselves secure in the keeping of nice, new, shiny gods they have just manufactured for themselves. *To a block of*

*wood they say: "Thou art my father" and to the stone "Thou
hast borne me."* The test will come when the sudden calamity comes and each man shall call frantically to his god for
help. That will be the hour of desperate need. What is the
good of a useless block of wood that must be carried when
the crying need is for one who can carry?

*The prophets prophesy falsely, the priests rule at
their bidding; and my people love it so. But what
will ye do when the end comes?* (5:31.)

In the hour of ease and soft living when prophets and
priests are false leaders and when the people love to have such
spineless leadership Jeremiah challenged them with this
startling question. It seems to be a desirable thing to have
such liberties when no trouble looms and when no one feels
any special need for the hand of God. Even prophets and
priests may show interest in pleasing men instead of God.
But in the tragic hour of distress and pain and death agony,
what will you do? In the light of present-day trends we may
well apply this question to our own hearts.

*Refuse silver shall men call them because Yahweh
has rejected them.* (6:30.)

When men reject God and begin losing the qualities of
mind and heart that provide charm and attractiveness it is
inevitable that they will be rejected of God. Why should
anyone desire them or keep them? Perhaps some day we may
see clearly how unattractive, how loathsome, how useless
sinful men are in the sight of a holy God. How we need to
look objectively at ourselves to see the miserable emptiness
that is so clearly visible to God! There is no point in keeping
refuse silver. It has no worth. Can it be that God has already
marked off as valueless many who consider themselves useful?

*What! Steal? Murder? Commit adultery? Burn in-
cense to Baal? Follow other gods? And then come*

and stand before me in this house and say, We are delivered in order to do all these abominations. Is this house, that is called by my name, become a den of robbers in your estimation? (7:8-11.)

The public religion of Jeremiah's day was organized hypocrisy thoroughly divorced from morality. Men whose lives were a violation of every law of God came into the Temple to satisfy some superstitious longing or through downright hypocrisy. It was the fixed purpose of God to destroy the Temple since it had become a symbol of false religion. They were setting the temple worship in the place of true devotion to Yahweh. Instead of making them better it covered their moral failures with the cloak of outward zeal and made them believe they were actually doing their part to please God.

These men were actual sinners against God and against their fellows. Theft, murder, adultery, perjury, superstitious worship of the Temple as having magical power, and a formal observance of religious teachings characterized their behavior. They revered an institution but ignored its ethics. Jesus came six hundred years later with the same high, ethical demands.

Obey my voice and I will be your God, and ye shall be my people: and walk ye in all the way that I command you. (7:23.)

Jeremiah anticipates by six hundred years the abolition of animal sacrifice. He is definitely set on leading the people to obey the ethical demands of Yahweh (cf. Hos. 6:6; I Sam. 15:22; I Cor. 1:17; Mic. 6:5-8). He goes so far as to say that the ark, the Temple, the tables of the Torah, the city of Jerusalem and the Jewish nation are unnecessary in the plan and purpose of God. The sacrificial system must go since it has come to take the place of genuine worship of God and since it is not an essential essence of religion. When it is a mere substitute for righteous conduct it is an abomination to God. He takes them back to the hour of the Exodus when God called for obedience and righteous behavior. It has ever been the call of God to His people. Jesus found the same emphasis needed when formalism, hypocrisy, superstition and open sin made a loathsome mixture that caused His sensitive heart to ache. He still asks us: *"Why call ye me Lord, Lord and do not the things which I say."*

> *Oh, that I had in the wilderness a travelers' lodging-place; then would I leave my people and go from them for they are all adulterers, an assembly of perfidious men. (9:2.)*

This verse reveals a glimpse of a tired, worn, discouraged prophet in one of his lowest moments. It might be called "a passing shadow on a great soul." In his hour of vexation he imagines he would like to break away from people who do not deserve anything of him. How sweet to be relieved of all responsibility and all irritations! He was literally sick of watching the empty, godless, formal substitute for religion. All his days he prayed, loved, preached and warned, only to find the sort of unresponsiveness that seared his soul. These people were doomed anyway. Why have to carry on at the killing pace? It is good to know that when Jeremiah had the privilege of leaving these same treacherous neighbors he chose to stay with them and give all the remaining days of his life doing his best with them.

> *Let not the wise man glory in his wisdom, nor the hero in his heroism. Let not the rich man glory in his wealth, but let him that glories glory in this, in understanding and knowing me, that I am the LORD. (9:23.)*

How may we make a nation great? Can it be that we are depending on false national securities? Jeremiah warns against reliance upon human *wisdom,* human *might,* and human *wealth*. These are all uncertain and unreliable and inadequate in the hour of crisis. If the nation would glory let it be sure of the central secret of national strength. Her people must *know* and *understand* and *lean on* the eternal God. In that way they may be sure of the boundless reservoir of strength for each emergency. Wisdom, might and riches will all be useful as they are put at the disposal of God. Righteousness, justice and loving-kindness will be woven into the warp and woof of the national structure. God, working through human hearts, will work wonders in the earth.

> *It is wood . . . the work of the hands . . . They deck*
> *it with silver . . . fasten it with nails . . . It must*
> *needs be carried . . . can do no harm . . . no good*
> *. . . but a stick of wood . . . falsehood . . . no breath*
> *in it.* (10:3-15.)

Jeremiah is cruel in his treatment of the poor, defenseless idols that men use as substitutes for God. They are unresponsive sticks that have to be decorated so as to conceal the fact that they are only dead wood. Instead of carrying they must be carried. They must be fashioned, God fashions. No speech, no power, no breath, no intelligence, no worth, no influence, and no permanence can be attributed to them. In contrast Yahweh is eternal, living, active, powerful. He creates, speaks, controls, influences, saves eternally. Why should men resort to false, useless works of mockery when they might have the constant presence of the eternal God? In the hour of supreme need the heart reaches out instinctively for satisfaction. Let that heart find the only genuine satisfaction in Yahweh of Hosts.

> *If thou hast run with the footmen and they have*
> *wearied thee, how canst thou contend with horses?*
> *What wilt thou do in the swelling of the Jordan?*
>
> (12:5.)

Jeremiah was complaining to God because of his hard lot. Yahweh strikes him with a terrific blow when He bluntly reminds him of trials, distresses and crises that are yet to come that will make his present irritations seem small. He assures His prophet that he knows and understands and gives credit for all of his past performances. He believes in Jeremiah and assures him that he is being chosen from the elementary training course to be promoted to the more difficult field of battle. Each bit of suffering he has endured has fitted him for new adventures. God does not throw us out into the race with horses until we have had training with footmen. Each victory we win will fit us to measure up in the hour of tragic crisis. What will *you* do in the swelling of the Jordan? When the Jordan bursts its banks how will you stand?

> *He was at work with the potter's wheels. Whenever the vessel he was making was spoiled he made of it another vessel, as it seemed good to the potter to do. Behold, as clay in the potter's hand, so are ye in my hand, says Yahweh.* (18:3, 4, 6.)

Jeremiah needed the lessons which the busy potter could teach him. He looked intently at the man, the clay and the wheels. The man was a specialist who was intelligently carrying out his purpose with capable material by means of the very best equipment available. He saw clearly a picture of God's sovereignty, His patience, His perseverance, His freedom, His resourcefulness and the effectiveness with which He carried out His eternal purpose. With perverse human clay in His hands he was unfettered by any previous decree or plan in His great task of molding human personality. Nothing in the clay could make a beautiful vessel of itself. The wheels could do nothing except as the hands of the potter worked. They were under the control of the potter. God is the supreme Figure and His purpose will ultimately be carried out. Man can mar God's plan because He has so graciously granted freedom of choice, but the infinite Potter will make it again as it seems good to Him.

> *Behold, I am against the prophets, says Yahweh. I sent them not. (23:30, 32.)*

With the coming of the Chaldeans the city was full of prophets who were busy with favorable predictions calculated to please the people. They were professionals who claimed to be speaking with divine authority but were actually giving utterance to lies and deceit. Jeremiah hurls three charges against them. He says they were actually immoral, that they did not know God, and that they had no message for the people. They were careless of sacred responsibilities and lowered the moral standards of the people by active participation in sin. Their knowledge of God was on a low plane. Not understanding His holy nature they thought and preached that He could not desert Israel. Jeremiah knew Him and understood His nature and knew that He must break away from people who had spurned Him.

These prophets clung to tradition and dogma along with the priests. Their messages were shallow and useless. No good could come to human hearts from them. The rebel Jeremiah sought truth fearlessly and recklessly and from his close touch with God was able to bring new truth, six hundred years ahead of his day.

> *Ye shall seek me, and find me, when ye shall search for me with all your heart. (29:13.)*

God's word to His people in the day of Jeremiah is still His sure word for men who have sinned and lost touch with the Infinite. No perfunctory gesture of interest can procure the rich treasure that is more valuable than all gold. He is always available. His longing is that all men may look to Him and live. His arms are always open in loving invitation to any who will turn to Him. It is just as true, however, that a diligent search is necessary. One who becomes conscious of his need, senses the satisfying gift of God, and sets out to find Him can be sure of victory if he seeks with his whole heart. Cleansing, peace, joy, victory will be his at the hand of a loving God who delights to welcome His children home.

I will make with them a new covenant, says Yahweh. I will put my law in their inward parts and on their heart will I write it. I will forgive their guilt, and their sin I will remember no more. (31:31, 33, 34.)

Jeremiah was familiar with the idea of religion based on a covenant. He saw that since the people had failed to recognize the reality of individual responsibility the old covenant had broken down. There was no hope of renewing the old covenant. A new one must be substituted for it. That covenant must be *personal, inward, universal, spiritual* and *efficacious.* The moral nature must be cleansed, God must be seen clearly, His will must be accurately apprehended. It is, therefore, to be a covenant of spiritual discernment, of divine fellowship, and of moral cleansing. We turn to Luke 22:14-20 for the highest fulfillment of this beautiful promise. Christ's new covenant relationship of grace was inaugurated as His solution for the problem which sin had created. The author of Hebrews (8, 9) describes this covenant as better in every particular since it sets up a worthy ideal with power to realize it, with an eternal High Priest instead of human priests, with a perfect sacrifice instead of animal victims, with realities instead of mere "shadows of things," with a perfect victory through the atoning death of the Lamb of God.

I will gather them . . . restore them . . . make them dwell safely . . . be their God . . . give them one heart . . . make an everlasting covenant with them . . . put my fear in their hearts . . . take delight in them . . . plant them in faithfulness.

(32:37-41.)

What a glorious picture of God's redeeming, restoring love! After the storm and the suffering the tender heart of God sends forth a strong arm to lift up, restore and set them securely in the chosen land again. The cleansing fire of exile will have done its part in burning out sinful elements and in welding them into one group of faithful followers of Yahweh. God's free forgiveness will make them eligible for an intimate relationship known and enjoyed by the favored few who have been granted such a precious privilege. The everlasting love of God is too vast to describe or explain. The issues of that love are too marvelous for our human comprehension.

PRACTICAL LESSONS OF PERMANENT VALUE

1. God's purpose includes the selection, the consecration, the calling and the empowering of an individual for His own hour.
2. Even a young, shrinking boy may be prepared by the touch of God to become a mighty messenger to sinning men.
3. Yahweh's tender heart is severely hurt by the sight of chosen ones who have forgotten the vows of honeymoon days.
4. Formal repetition of pious phrases and the offering of costly sacrifices are but an insult to God.
5. God never calls men to run with horses until He has subjected them to easier training with footmen.
6. Sin is a thing of the heart and must be dealt with by the divine Surgeon who goes directly to the source for it.
7. Genuine repentance must precede the giving of God's blessings in individual lives.
8. True religion is an inward, spiritual, genuine response of the heart to the righteous God.
9. The way to power is still found in a deep, personal experience with the Infinite.

10. Sin always results in ruin. Judgment is inevitable, automatic and eternal.

11. Religion may be tested by its results in producing the right sort of conduct and attitudes.

12. Sin cannot triumph, for God must have the ultimate victory over evil.

13. Each man stands alone before a righteous God and must be judged as an individual soul.

14. The new covenant provides for a divine operation on the human heart that true life may be guaranteed.

15. The minister who suffers most and leans most heavily on God is the one who knows the deeper truths of God.

16. God confers a signal honor upon His prophet when He calls him into that intimate relationship which gives daily guidance and strength for all the hard places.

ʹʹʹ HABAKKUK ʹʹʹ

In "Paracelsus" Robert Browning says:

> *If I stoop*
> *Into a dark tremendous sea of cloud,*
> *It is but for a time; I press God's lamp*
> *Close to my breast; its splendor, soon or late,*
> *Will pierce the gloom: I shall emerge one day.*

It is sometimes difficult to understand and justify God's ways. Habakkuk was greatly perplexed and worried over the confused issues about him, as men today are confused and bewildered. Why does God allow the devastating ruin to go unchecked? Why does a whole world have to continue to suffer while ungodly criminals plunge us deeper into the abyss? When will God lift His hand to change the tide and cause justice to reign on the earth? The careful study of the message of Habakkuk will help toward a sane solution of questions that have baffled men for centuries.

THE TIMES

The prophet had witnessed the reformation under the dynamic leadership of Josiah, the last good king of Judah. He watched the fading glow of the setting sun of Assyria. A great world kingdom was dying before his eyes. Egypt and Babylon were fighting to take the place of the departing lord. In a vain attempt to frustrate the plans of Necho of Egypt Josiah was killed at Megiddo. The issue was finally decided in 605 B.C. when Nebuchadrezzar of Babylon drove the Egyptians back in defeat and took over the civilized world as his kingdom. As Habakkuk saw such mighty up-heavals and realized the tragic consequences of the struggles that were going on around him, he was greatly perplexed.

He probably wrote the book about the time of the fall of the city of Nineveh in 612 B.C. or within the next few years before the actual victory of Babylon in 605 B.C.

Tyranny and strife and lawlessness were rife in Judah. Men raised up strife and contention (1:1), oppressed righteous people (1:2, 13), lived in open sin (2:4, 5, 15, 16), worshiped idols (2:18, 19), oppressed the poor and the defenseless (1:4, 14, 15). It was a dark day of sin, strife, lawlessness and imminent invasion. Greater disasters seemed to be in store for God's people in Jerusalem.

THE MAN

Very little is known of Habakkuk except that which comes from a thoughtful study of his words. Evidently he was a prominent citizen of Jerusalem who had the confidence and respect of the leaders of the city. He has been called the "freethinker among the prophets" and the "father of Israel's religious doubt," but we must realize that he was a man of clear faith and powerful hold on God. In a sense he is a spokesman for Israel to God. In spite of his strong faith, the facts of life were too much for him. He could not get his questions answered. A man of reverent spirit, with keen, sensitive, highly developed faculties, he was more seriously troubled than any other man in the kingdom.

Ward says of him: "He was given a recognized place among those who had received the oracles of God, and he assuredly is one of the finest writers in the Old Testament. The beauty of his language and his chaste style entitle him to a place in the front rank of the prophetic school." [1]

Robinson says of him: "He was a philosopher, earnest and candid, and possessed of unusual originality and force, sensitive, speculative, the suppliant among the prophets, and the preacher of theocratic optimism." [2]

He was a careful student of God's dealings with His chosen

[1] *Ibid.*, p. 226.
[2] *Ibid.*, p. 119.

people through the years. The words and works of Amos, Hosea, Micah and Isaiah were familiar to him. The precepts and promises given in the Law of Moses formed the basis for much that he said. In addition he was a careful student of life and the experience of men. It was at this point that his most serious problems arose, for he had great difficulty in harmonizing the rich promises and the dire threats of God with the actual happenings of his daily observation.

When his doubts arose and he could not reconcile a bad world with a good God and a righteous law, he refused utterly to dismiss his doubts without an answer. He was honest and fearless and dogged in his determination to find the solution to the perplexing and conflicting problem. We thank God for an honest searcher after truth who was willing to go directly to God for the answer.

THE BOOK

Habakkuk arranges his book in the form of a dramatic dialogue between the prophet and Yahweh. There follows a series of woes against the cruel Chaldeans and a beautiful poem expressing confidence in the God of his salvation.

1. *The prophet's passionate protest* (1:2-4). Why does God allow the wicked and lawless men of Judah to continue unpunished? How long will God allow the injustice, the brutality, the wrong to go on in Jerusalem? It is a definite complaint to God.

2. *The first answer of Yahweh* (1:5-11). God refuses to admit that he is inattentive or inactive or indifferent. He challenges his prophet to look beyond the limited borders of Israel. He is already working a work. He has already enlisted the Chaldeans in the work of chastising the people of Jerusalem. They are cruel, swift, deadly instruments who will cause a tragic scourge to sweep over the land. Judgment will come upon Judah.

3. *The moral problem* (1:12-17). The prophet has complained of God's indifference. He is now horrified to hear

the means God is using to bring about His purpose on Israel.
How can God use such a cruel instrument to scourge Judah?
How can a righteous God use the Chaldeans to punish his
own neighbors and friends? How can He reconcile the cruelty and inhumanity of the enemy with His own purity and
holiness? It is a real problem that confronts the pious old
prophet. He boldly challenges God to defend His actions:

> *Thou that art of purer eyes than to behold evil, and*
> *that canst not look on perverseness, wherefore dost*
> *thou look upon them that deal treacherously, and*
> *holdest thy peace when the wicked swallows up the*
> *man who is more righteous than he?* (1:13.)

4. *An important decision* (2:1). The prophet finds the
solution only when he obediently takes his place on the
watchtower to wait expectantly for the true revelation from
God. The world is in ruins about him and the hosts of
Chaldea are coming to help destroy what is left, but he is
finding the one source of solution to his problems. Rever-
ently and expectantly he watches for the answer from God.

5. *God's second reply* (2:2-4). The deeper solution now
follows. He admits the wickedness of the Chaldeans but declares that they will perish by the very explosive power of
evil. The divine purpose is moving gradually but surely on
to its certain fulfillment. Cruelty and pride must be destroyed, righteousness must triumph. The present situation
requires patience. God does not feel any need for hurry.

> *Though the mills of God grind slowly,*
> *Yet they grind exceedingly small:*
> *Though with patience He stands waiting,*
> *With exactness grinds He all.*[3]

Harrell says: "God has all the ages in which to demonstrate
his justice. The testing of time will reveal what men are, as
fire separates gold from the dross. The Chaldeans may pros-

[3] Longfellow, *Retribution*.

per in their wickedness for a season, and seem to triumph over a people more righteous than they. Yet they carry in themselves 'the germs of certain ruin.' The years, which are the crucible of God, will make manifest the essential weakness of an ungodly people." [4]

Robinson says: "The future belongs to the righteous; whereas, those whose souls are *puffed up* and arrogant have no future! The Chaldeans are self-centered, and are therefore doomed; the righteous are God-centered and are therefore permanent." [5]

6. *A series of five woes* (2:5-20). The haughty conqueror is described and condemned. The indictment is terrific. 5-8, the lust for land and possessions. 9-11, the covetous desire for selfish gain. 12-14, the oppression that takes cities and buildings. 15-17, the godless banquets where God is dishonored and helpless people suffer. 18-20 the silly, irrational, foolish worship of idols. Before the unfolding of the divine glory all evil must perish. The criminals of Chaldea will be destroyed along with all others who oppose the will of Yahweh.

7. *A beautiful anthem of praise* (3:1-19). This poem has been called "Habakkuk's Pindaric Ode." Robinson says: "It is bold in conception, sublime in thought, majestic in diction, and pure in rhetoric." [6] After a fervent prayer the prophet is rewarded with an appearance of God himself. Through all the years God has been faithful and has responded to the cry for help that came from His followers. Each crisis has been met by the sovereign God who has revealed His infinite power. As the prophet looks he sees the onward march of God through the centuries and realizes that the same active God is in control and that He is working out His own purpose in His own good time. Even though disaster and destruction and ruin await him, Habakkuk comes to realize

[4] *Ibid.*, p. 113.
[5] *Ibid.*, p. 123.
[6] *Ibid.*, p. 125.

that he can trust implicitly in Yahweh. He sees that only a small part of God's plan is visible at the time and that God would have him wait patiently for the fuller revelation.

> *For though the fig-tree shall not flourish,*
> *Neither shall fruit be on the vines,*
> *The labor of the olive shall fail,*
> *And the fields shall yield no food;*
> *The flock shall be cut off from the fold,*
> *And there shall be no herd in the stalls:*
> *Yet I will rejoice in Yahweh,*
> *I will joy in the God of my salvation.* (3:17f.)

Ward says: "Out of his doubts, the prophet forged a new belief in the character of the Infinite. Against the dark background of human hatred, greed and aggression, stood forth the pure presence of the All-Holy. Where before he had been on the brink of despair, like a traveller lost in the trackless desert, like a shipwrecked mariner dying of thirst, now circumstances were subordinated to faith. We are the offspring of God. We are meant not for the valley of fears, but for the high place of faith; not for the slough of Despond, but for the Delectable mountains with their glimpse of the celestial city and the good yet to be!" [7]

Practical Lessons of Permanent Value

1. God never stifles a sincere questioner.
2. Some problems cannot have a definite, direct answer.
3. In every crisis God can be trusted.
4. The short view is apt to be the false view.
5. When faith is swept off its feet it finds that it has wings.
6. Evil has within itself the germs of death.
7. We may see and understand God only when we rise above the fog of human doubt.

[7] *Ibid.,* pp. 239, 241.

8. It helps us to understand something of the vast sympathy of God.

9. The real purpose of religion is not to have all doubts solved, but to be sure of God.

10. In dealing with doubt God invites us to turn to Him and wait for His answer.

11. Remember these verses:

> *The righteous shall live by faith* (2:4.)
> *Woe to him that buildeth a town with blood*
> (2:12.)
> *The Lord is in His holy temple: let all the earth keep silence before Him* (2:20.)
> *For the earth shall be filled with the knowledge of the glory of Yahweh, as the waters cover the sea* (2:14.)

··· NAHUM ···

IN A DAY WHEN DICTATORS ARE SEEKING TO RUN RUTHLESSLY
over the whole earth, the prophet Nahum comes to us with
peculiar freshness and meaning. Vengeance still belongs to
God. Such monstrous disregard of God and His righteous
standards will bring swift and certain judgment. Any nation
that deliberately sets itself to defy God and trample upon innocent peoples must feel the terrible touch of the divine
hand. Professor Kennedy calls Assyria "an object lesson to
the empires of the modern world, teaching as an eternal prin-
ciple of the divine government of the world, the absolute
necessity, for a nation's continued vitality, of that righteousness—personal, civic and national—which alone exalteth a
nation." [1] Nahum's book is a terrific arraignment of a nation
that seeks glory by war and oppression. God still hates brutality, violence and wrong.

THE TIMES

Nahum lived and preached sometime between the fall of
Thebes in 663 B.C. and the fall of Nineveh in 612 B.C. George
Adam Smith puts the date of the book at 640 B.C. while the
majority of recent scholars tend to date it much nearer the
time of Nineveh's collapse.

Esarhaddon, who reigned in Nineveh fro.n 681–669 B.C.,
did much to build a great kingdom. Egypt was conquered
and made a part of his empire. Assurbanipal, 669–626 B.C.,
continued the work of his illustrious father throughout a
long and stormy reign. His interest in beautiful palaces and
in great libraries caused him to spend his time and energy in
establishing himself as "the greatest known patron of literature in the pre-Christian centuries."

[1] Hastings' Bible Dictionary.

At his death in 626 B.C. an enemy of Assyria, Nabopolassar became king of the Babylonians. The death knell of Assyria was thus sounded. Nineveh could hold out for some years but her mighty empire was doomed. The Medes under Cyaxares and the bloodthirsty Scythians joined forces with the enemies of Nineveh to bring about her ruin.

Nineveh, founded by Nimrod, had been famous for centuries. With walls one hundred feet high, seven and one half miles in circumference, and wide enough for three chariots to drive abreast, the city presented a formidable front to any invader. It also boasted twelve hundred defense towers and a moat outside the walls one hundred and forty feet wide and sixty feet deep. The destruction of the city was so complete that Alexander the Great did not notice the site in 331 B.C. It was 1842 before a trace of the city was discovered by Layard and Botta.

In 612 B.C. the city fell never to rise again. The pomp and pride and glory of the mighty mistress of the world were brought low. A new world power arose to dominate the peoples of the earth.

In Jerusalem Manasseh reigned from 698 B.C. until about 643 B.C. His son Amon ruled only two years and then the youthful Josiah began his eventful reign. Jeremiah and Zephaniah were preaching in Jerusalem. Huldah was a prophetess of influence with the king and the people. In 623 B.C. the reformation under Josiah's leadership caused a great change in the life of the nation. When the Book of the Law was found and read to the people they set out to clean up the land and set up the sort of worship it described. The reformation lacked spiritual depth but it did bring about a new emphasis on the requirements of God's law.

THE MAN

The name Nahum means "consolation" or "compassion." We do not know where he lived. Some have contended that his home was at Elkosh on the banks of the Tigris river.

Jerome claimed that he was a native of Galilee living near
Capernaum ("city of Nahum"). Kennedy would make him a
resident of a small village near Micah's home in southwest
Judah.

Nahum was a patriotic saint, who had a deep hatred for
the Assyrians. His sensitive nature, strained almost to the
breaking point by the godless cruelty of the inhuman warriors, was almost fanatical in his exultation over the horrible
suffering of the enemy. He was keenly observant. To him the
seas, the hills, the storms, the clouds and the river were
symbols of God's wrath and fury. His quick imagination,
coupled with his keen intuition, made him a vivid painter
with words. His sense of a holy God so tragically outraged
by unscrupulous men drove him to lengths unreached by
others. As a poet he has few equals. His soul, on fire with
righteous indignation, flashed and blazed in dramatic poetry.

THE BOOK

The theme. On every page is evident the vivid picture of
the impending doom of Nineveh. The judgment of the Lord
though long deferred is sure and final. Vengeance belongs to
God. Yahweh is against any nation that acquires wealth and
glory by oppression and slaughter and war. Farley says: "He
speaks in the name of outraged humanity, cowed and tor-
mented by the brutal cruelty of Assyria." [2]

The style. For sheer beauty, poetic imagery, dramatic
description and vivid imagination Nahum is unsurpassed
among the prophets. He describes the swift, relentless sweep
of the enemy with all the vividness and color of an eye witness. G. A. Smith says: "His language is strong and brilliant;
his rhythm rumbles and rolls, leaps and flashes, like the
horsemen and chariots he describes." [3] He was charged with
emotion. His whole being was under the spell of a mighty
torrent of feeling.

[2] *Ibid.*, p. 112.
[3] *Ibid.*, p. 90.

De Wette says: "It is a classic in all respects. It is marked by clearness, by its finished elegance, as well as by fire, richness and originality. The rhythm is regular and lively." [4] Brice calls it "the most vivid and passionate fragment of declamation in all literature." [5]

The outline.

Chapter 1   A sublime picture of God.
Chapter 2   A graphic picture of the fall of Nineveh.
Chapter 3   A statement of the reasons for the utter ruin of the wicked city.

Morgan gives the following: [6]

Chapter 1   The *Verdict* of Vengeance.
Chapter 2   The *Vision* of Vengeance.
Chapter 3   The *Vindication* of Vengeance.

Scroggie states it as follows: [7]

Chapter 1   Judgment on Nineveh *declared.*
Chapter 2   Judgment on Nineveh *described.*
Chapter 3   Judgment on Nineveh *defended.*

GREAT RELIGIOUS IDEAS

It is good to be reminded that the eternal God is still in active control of the affairs of His world. His sovereign will is to hold sway to the ends of the earth. When He lifts His finger in judgment the mightiest nation with the most elaborate equipment is doomed to fall. His patience with arrogant aggressors cannot continue always.

Nahum gave emphasis to the eternal truth that world kingdoms founded on selfishness, greed, force and treachery must be completely destroyed. He was just as clear on the doctrine that God's kingdom, built upon truth, righteous-

[4] Quoted by Scroggie. *Know Your Bible* (vol. 1), p. 180.
[5] *Ibid.,* p. 49.
[6] *Ibid.,* p. 72.
[7] *Ibid.,* p. 183.

ness and integrity, has within itself the very seeds of permanence. To him the land of Judah was Yahweh's land. Any oppressor of Judah was an active enemy of her God. When Yahweh destroyed Nineveh He was merely bringing upon His own enemy the punishment so richly deserved.

Nahum was sure of the existence of a moral order that could be depended upon to set justice in the earth. No nation could transgress the great conceptions of ethical religion with impunity. God had prepared a higher court to guarantee a square deal for every nation and every individual. Retribution was certain.

Nahum does not ask Judah to repent, though he certainly recognizes her need for such repentance. He is primarily concerned with his one message concerning the doom of Nineveh and the triumph of God's retributive righteousness. He does not seem to recognize that the cruel oppressors who deliver the death blow to the capital of Assyria will be just as cruel and godless in their treatment of the neighboring peoples. Definitely set to denounce the Assyrians, he makes it clear that God is opposed to the kind of behavior that Nineveh has practiced and that such behavior will always bring swift retribution. Such sins bring an automatic punishment.

Such a message must have brought hope to hearts that were clinging to God in troublous times. He could be depended upon to set justice in the earth and to reward those who were faithful to Him. It is a comforting thought that comes to us from the fiery pages of this "hymn of hate." Throughout the book we see the true nature of God as a tender, compassionate Being shining behind the tragic exhibition of His wrath. It is because of His tender love that His anger blazes so fiercely.

PRACTICAL LESSONS OF PERMANENT VALUE

1. There is a limit to the patience of God.
2. God is in active control throughout all the world.

3. God's wrath must be interpreted in terms of His love.
4. For nations and for individuals *the wages of sin is death.*
5. The arrogance that indulges in senseless destruction of life and property angers God.
6. A nation built on pride, cruelty, force, and selfishness, cannot hope to have friends in the day of calamity.
7. In God's eternal purpose for the people of the world the destruction of one wicked city is but a small thing.
8. In the day of distress and anguish men who do not have a grip on God must suffer untold sufferings.

‚‚‚ ZEPHANIAH ‚‚‚

THE PROPHETS REPRESENTED GOD AS BOTH SEVERE AND
tender. His nature expresses itself in contrasting ways. Severity and tenderness are constantly manifesting themselves
as we watch the divine dealings with men. This contrast is
especially clear in the message of Zephaniah. He presents the
terror and the tenderness of divine love.

In 1:2 God says:

*I will utterly consume all things from off the face
of the ground.*

In 1:2 and 3:17 he says:

*The Lord thy God is in the midst of thee, a mighty
One who will save; he will rest in His love, he will
joy over thee with singing.*

THE BACKGROUND

Zephaniah lived in an hour of decay and dissolution in
the midst of a rapidly changing world order. The savage
horde of Scythians pouring down from the plains of South
Russia threw fear and consternation into the hearts of the
peoples of Palestine. They were cruel, bloodthirsty, fearless,
ruthless ruffians who drove relentlessly on as far as Egypt.
Their merciless behavior created a panic in the hearts of
men. The great Assyrian power that had held absolute sway
since the rise of Tiglath Pileser in 745 B.C. was fast losing its
hold in the world. When Assurbanipal died in 626 B.C. the
death knell of Assyria was sounded. The powerful Babylonian kingdom under Nabopolassar, was now in position to
take over the supremacy of the East. Nineveh was not destroyed until 612 B.C. but from 626 B.C. Babylon was really
the mistress of the nations. The union of the armies of the

Medes, the Scythians and the Babylonians caused a mighty upheaval in the world. It is not a small thing to watch the death of one world empire and the coming into life of another. As a young man Zephaniah witnessed these epoch-making happenings.

Josiah came to the throne in Jerusalem following the death of Manasseh and Amon. It would be difficult to describe the tragic effects of the long reign of Manasseh. The nation was converted into heathenism, with foreign fashions, practices, worship and behavior the order of the day. The pure worship of Yahweh was banished. The effect of the lower ethical standards showed up in the behavior of the people. The princes of Judah had become so corrupt that justice was impossible. Injustice, oppression and violence were the natural results of the sort of court life that Josiah found. He could not hope to do much as a lad in the midst of a group that had thrown off restraints and turned pagan. Two generations had grown up since the good days of Isaiah and Hezekiah. No prophets had been allowed to speak of the deep things of God. The entire life of the court was opposed to the sort of preaching that God's chosen prophet would bring. The people had been stimulated by so many false things that they had become callous to any stimulus. They were "settled on their lees." In Zephaniah's indictment of Jerusalem he pictures the people as unteachable, the rulers as predatory, the courts as merciless, the prophets as traitors, and the priests as profane. It was a dark day for God's land.

Josiah set out to clean up the Temple and to turn the people back to Yahweh worship. In the course of the repairs on the Temple a book was found that made a profound impression on king and people. The book was a part of the Pentateuch that gave directions for the behavior of God's people in the chosen land. The youthful king realized at once something of the significance of the book. Huldah, the prophetess, was consulted and God's word was brought to the king. As a result of the reading of the Law a definite effort at reform was undertaken. Idols, images, groves, high places, pagan altars and other abominations were broken down. An effort was made to force upon the people a nation-wide reform. It was a great undertaking and did much for the kingdom. It failed only in that the reforms could not go deep enough to transform individual hearts and lives. Outwardly it was a great success. Too much credit cannot be given to the zealous young king.

We cannot be sure what part Zephaniah and Jeremiah played in the reform movement. They were both vitally interested in cleaning up the land and in a genuine turning to God. Jeremiah was quite young and probably lacked the sort of leadership that would give him much influence with the people. We may be sure that Zephaniah and Jeremiah encouraged Josiah in his worthy ambitions and that they helped as far as possible in stirring up the people to carry out the king's orders. It is perhaps best to date the activities of Zephaniah from 625 B.C.

THE MAN

The Hebrew prophets were usually in sympathy with the poor so that their messages became strong indictments of the nobles who possessed wealth and lands. Zephaniah was an aristocrat who did not pose as a spokesman of the peasant. With justifiable pride he traced his lineage back to Hezekiah. It must have given him standing with princes and rulers as he stepped out to proclaim his stern denunciations. He was probably the same age as Josiah and Jeremiah.

His book reveals an exceptionally accurate knowledge of Jerusalem itself. He must have spent all his days in that city. His grim, austere, sober nature has gained for him the name "puritan" or "protestant." He seemed obsessed with a terrible conception of the doom that was coming upon the wicked world about him. No hope was in sight, for the certain doom was richly deserved and must come on friend and foe alike.

He had a comprehensive view of history. One is tempted to speculate on the type of educational institutions that prepared young men in the way so many of the prophets were educated. Zephaniah reminds us of Isaiah in his broad understanding of the guilt and needs of other nations. He thought of his civilization as incurably corrupt. All the surrounding nations were equally enmeshed in sin and guilt. His own beloved land was involved and must suffer the cruel tortures of a just God who could do no other thing in the light of men's behavior. Yahweh was to sweep away, as with a devastating flood, all the nations; and Judah must suffer the full severity of the onslaught. A new era of peace, plenty and happiness was to follow in the wake of the destruction.

Zephaniah was not a poet. He was deeply impressed with the fact that God had laid His hand on him and that he must warn his beloved people of the impending calamity. He was sensitive to the faintest whisper of God. Imagination and emotion play a large place in his preaching. He was a flaming evangelist who spoke with fury and effectiveness a burning message of rebuke to a people who were rapidly losing all power to respond to such serious challenges. Being violently opposed to world conditions he left the impression that he was pitiless and harsh and unsympathetic. Some have called him fanatical. However this may be, he was vitally concerned with the proclamation of the divine denunciation.

THE BOOK

Zephaniah's book is made up of several brief oracles delivered during the early days of Josiah's preparation for the reformation. In scathing language he announces the coming day of wrath and destruction for all who have sinned against the holy God of hosts.

In the opening paragraph he pronounces certain doom on all those who are worshiping idols. Heathenism and idolatry must be purged from the land. Yahweh cannot allow such abominations to live. In 1:7-13 the rulers are denounced along with every class of sinner. 1:14-18 pictures God's wrath bringing a blast of fire upon the whole earth but striking with peculiar fury upon the inhabitants of Jerusalem. The *Day of Yahweh* is a dread day of retribution. Let all the peoples tremble in the presence of the God of Israel.

In chapter two the prophet begins with an urgent call to repentance (2:1-3) that they may be *hid in the day of the Lord's anger*. Nothing can avert the doom on the nation, but genuine repentance may save the praying remnant. He then (2:4-15) turns upon the heathen nations, Philistia, Moab, Ammon, Ethiopia and Assyria with dire threats of destruction. In the day of His wrath Yahweh will leave no nation unpunished.

In chapter three the prophet returns to his native city with a stinging threat. Judah has been obstinate and rebellious. He sets her sins out in the light of Yahweh's righteousness and holiness. The appeal to his neighbors to repent seems to fall on dull ears. He then assures them that a hidden remnant will survive the overflowing scourge and be safe in the protection of their God. These saved ones are to be the friends of God after the purging that will fit them for His presence. The promise of salvation to the world through this divinely preserved remnant is a characteristic doctrine of the spiritual prophets. Zephaniah pleads for patience until a double-edged consequence can be found. The heathen are to be judged and destroyed while Judah is to have a holy remnant that will remain to enjoy the rich blessings of their God. The redeemed remnant will return with their offerings to Zion, and be planted there to the undoing of transgression. When they are fully established in the land with Yahweh in their midst, Zion shall be a praise in the earth and a delight among the nations. These songs of deliverance and rejoicing bring a fitting close to the book.

The most beautiful part of the book is 3:11-13. The most

valuable part is probably 1:2-2:3 and 3:1-13. The prophecies against foreign nations in 2:4-15 reveal a narrow nationalistic spirit that fails to measure up to the best.

Some one has given the following brief outline of the book:

1:1-18   A declaration of retribution.

2:1-3:8   An exhortation to repentance.

3:8-20   A promise of redemption.

PRACTICAL LESSONS OF PERMANENT VALUE

1. A man's belief about God largely determines his conduct.

2. It is universally true that one tends to become like the God he worships.

3. Living a life is serious business and should call out the best and most serious endeavor.

4. The wrath of God is a terrible thing when turned upon human sin.

5. Earnest warning is sorely needed to draw us back to the presence of God.

6. The Day of Yahweh is inevitable for all men of every race.

7. God gives assurance that the humble ones who seek Him will be safe in His presence in the day of destruction.

8. God's ministers should put strong emphasis upon the spiritual nature of God's kingdom.

9. The promise that joy will displace mourning and tranquillity will follow the storm, should bring joy to sorrowing hearts.

10. God's purpose is not to wreak vengeance but to cleanse and refine and save those who will allow Him to save them.

⁗ OBADIAH ⁗

THE PROPHECY OF OBADIAH IS THE SHORTEST BOOK IN THE
Old Testament. It is directed against the people of Edom
who looked on while Jerusalem was being plundered and
who manifested fiendish delight in the misfortune that over-
took her inhabitants. George Adam Smith calls it "an indignant oration."

THE LAND OF EDOM

The story of a venomous family feud that takes us back to
the days of Jacob and Esau is unfolded before our eyes.
Esau's descendants settled in Edom, a land to the south of
the Dead Sea about one hundred miles long and fifty miles
wide. Living on these well-watered plains the Edomites could
drive shrewd trades, make raids on neighboring peoples and
retreat to their impregnable strongholds for safety. Sela
(Petra), Teman, and Bozrah were the fortified citadels that
served as places of security in war.

Petra was one of the wonders of the world. With massive
cliffs more than seven hundred feet high sheltering a narrow
ravine a mile in length, the city was able to repel any invasion. Being on an important caravan route it became a
trading center that had few equals. The buildings of pink
stone carved out of solid rock still stand, to the amazement of
all visitors. The purple cliffs of iron and manganese make
a background that defies description.

The Edomites refused to allow the Israelites passage
through their territory at the time of the Exodus (Num. 20).
In the battle for the conquest of Palestine they fought against
Israel. David subdued the land and Solomon continued to
hold it in subjection. In the days of Ahaz the Edomites rebelled and continued to make trouble for Judah throughout
the remaining days of the kingdom. Judas Maccabaeus drove

them out of Southern Judah in 164 B.C. John Hyrcanus later
forced them to accept Judaism. They became the hated
Idumeans of the New Testament days and gave to the Jews
the Herod family. After the destruction of Jerusalem in
70 A.D. they disappeared from history.

Harrell says of the Edomites: "Since the day when Jacob
by cunning became possessor of his brother's birthright the
children of Esau and the children of Jacob had been on bad
terms. Family feuds are long and bitter and tragic. Moreover,
between the Edomites and the Hebrews there was a funda-
mental difference in genius and character. The general
characteristics of Esau and Jacob ran in their blood. The
Edomites, like their father Esau, were a fleshly-minded
people, having no appreciation of the unseen and no dreams
for the future. They lived for food, spoil, and vengeance,
with no national conscience or ideals. It is significant that
nowhere in the Old Testament is any mention made of the
gods of the Edomites. They doubtless had their gods, as other
nations, but their deities must have been exceedingly drab
and unappealing; for Israel, continually fascinated by the
idolatries of her friends and foes, does not so much as intimate that Edom had a religion." [1]

The Prophet

Nothing is known of the author of these twenty-one verses
beyond the picture we find in his words. Obadiah is a common name in the Old Testament and Delitzsch suggests that
the man sent out by Jehoshaphat as a teacher of the people
was probably the writer of these lines (II Chron. 17:7). The
name means "worshiper of Yahweh" or "servant of Yahweh"
according to the vocalization of the word.

We know from the temper of his book that he was a pious,
patriotic, sensitive resident of Judah who dared put into
words something of the flaming indignation of his soul. He
was hurt by the serious lack of ordinary decency displayed

[1] *Ibid.*, p. 166.

by his neighbors. In biting words he denounced these proud sinners who deserved all the punishment that God was about to heap upon them. He seemed to be thoroughly willing to wait for God to take His own time to destroy the old strongholds for he had faith to believe that Yahweh would bring about a glorious victory and that right would triumph over wrong. His prophecy is saved from serious criticism by the spirit manifested in the closing verse:

The kingdom shall be Yahweh's.

THE BOOK

The theme of his book is the utter destruction of Edom. Nothing can save the guilty nation. Rock fortresses, impregnable cities, narrow mountain gorges, proud warriors cannot avail, for Yahweh has already decreed her destruction. Her craft is to be baffled, her rich storehouses plundered, her power broken, her pride humbled and her name forgotten. God is ready to make an end of her sordid selfishness, her love of wrong, her treachery, her hate, her arrogance and her vaunted security.

The occasion and date. What caused such an outbreak against Edom? Why should Obadiah be so bitter in his denunciation? In the tragic hour when the city was being plundered and sacked he had recently seen the Edomites display an inhuman spirit toward the people of Judah. While marauders did their worst these neighboring kinsmen displayed an unbrotherly spirit by their fiendish delight at Jerusalem's calamity. They helped catch fleeing Israelites, treated them cruelly, sold them as slaves, and shared in the loot obtained after the capture of the city

When did this attack on Jerusalem take place? It is spoken of as

the day of distress, the day of their calamity, the day of their destruction.

There were at least five invasions of Jerusalem that caused

havoc to the city and its inhabitants. Shishak of Egypt came against it in the days of Rehoboam. The Philistines and Arabians damaged the city during the reign of Jehoram. Jehoash of Israel took it in the days of Amaziah. Rezin of Damascus and Pekah of Israel captured the city before Tiglath Pileser could come to the aid of Ahaz. Nebuchadrezzar destroyed it and carried the people away in 587 B.C.

In considering a date for the book we can narrow this list down to two attacks—the one in the days of Jehoram, 845 B.C., and the other the final capture of Jerusalem in 587 B.C. Obadiah is either the earliest of the writing prophets or he prepared his book after the fall of Jerusalem. It would be much easier to think of the book as finding its occasion in Nebuchadrezzar's capture of the city were it not for the passages in Jeremiah that are almost certainly quoted from Obadiah. Jeremiah's words concerning Edom found in 49:7-22 contain several direct quotations from the Book of Obadiah or both of the prophets are quoting from an earlier source. If these words of Jeremiah were delivered in the early days of Jehoiakim it would seem to be certain that Obadiah's prophecy was delivered before the tragic destruction of the city. It may be best to follow Kirkpatrick, Delitzsch and Orelli in the assumption that Obadiah is describing the behavior of the Edomites when Jerusalem was sacked by the Arabians and Philistines in the reign of Jehoram, 848-844 B.C. On this theory Obadiah would be the earliest of the writing prophets.

Wellhausen contended that verses 10-14 describe the attitude of Edom at the fall of Jerusalem while verses 1-9 describe what has already happened to Edom instead of a prediction of future doom. He thought the date for the completion of the book was near the end of the fifth century. Farley says: "Verses 1-9 (or 10) are pre-Exilic and borrowed from an older source, while verses 11-21 are Exilic or post-Exilic." [2] Kirkpatrick says: "there is much to be said in favor of the unity of the Book of Obadiah. It forms a symmetrical whole. The doom of Edom is naturally followed by the reason for that doom, while the promise of the restoration of Judah forms the natural counterfoil to the fate of Edom, and an appropriate conclusion to the prophecy." [3]

The Outline.

1-9   Edom must be destroyed.

10-14 The reasons for the destruction,—cruelty, treachery and unbrotherly conduct.

15-21 In the hour of judgment Edom will be ruined while Israel will be restored and blessed.

PRACTICAL LESSONS OF PERMANENT VALUE

In this brief book we cannot hope to find a great amount of preaching material. It may be that one would pass over it entirely with the thought that such indignant words could hardly hold lessons of value for us. In its verses, however, we find a strong denunciation of the callous indifference of the man who stands aloof in the hour of distress and calamity without lifting a hand to help his brother. It is a strong word of warning against enmity, hatred, envy, and unbrotherly conduct. Pusey calls the crime "malicious gazing on human calamity, forgetful of man's common origin and common liability to ill, which is the worst form of human hate. It was one of the contumelies of the cross 'They gaze, they look with joy upon me'." [4]

Obadiah believed that God is in active control of every phase of His creation and that He has the universe framed on the law of righteousness. He was certain of the inflexible integrity of God. It was God's joy to carry out His purpose upon all the nations and to look with special favor upon His chosen people.

[3] *Ibid.,* p. 39.
[4] Quoted by Farley, *The Progress of Prophecy,* p. 208. Used by permission of the publishers Fleming H. Revell.

1. Human defenses are utterly useless when the power of God comes against them.
2. Ridicule is always bad for it reveals a low human pride that means an utter lack of brotherly love.
3. God can be depended upon to reveal His righteous purpose in His own good time.
4. Eternal justice will prevail.
5. *Pride goeth before destruction and a haughty spirit before a fall.*
6. The profane person cannot expect to find favor at the hand of the God whom he has never loved.
7. It is criminal to rejoice in the calamity of another and to gloat over his misfortune.
8. *The kingdom shall be Yahweh's.* It is great to know that the victory is to be God's victory.
9. Cadman says: "It teaches us that hate silences the voice of compassion, blinds the soul's vision, corrupts the social fabric, inflicts needless grief and dismay on innocent multitudes, and consigns the political systems founded it to self-wrought destruction.—No nationalism is defensible if it presumes to limit either God's love and righteousness or our own moral obligations." [5]

⁵ *Ibid.*, p. 149.

''' EZEKIEL '''

THE FAITHFUL PREACHER TO THE EXILES IN BABYLON MAKES
a special appeal to the ministers of any generation. His
method, his earnestness, his style, his peculiar effectiveness,
and his gripping message will help them deal with the people
to whom they minister. For twenty-two years (593-571 B.C.)
he dealt with discouraged captives who needed a strong
leader.

THE TIMES

In Jerusalem (598-587 B.C.) the people of Israel lived in
constant trouble. Johoiakim was succeeded by his son Jehoiachin who reigned only three months before being taken to
Babylon along with the best of all the people of Judah.
Ezekiel was taken in this group of 10,000 captives. The
temple treasures, the artisans, the soldiers, the princes and
everything else of value found lodgment in Babylon. Zedekiah was left on the throne in Jerusalem as the agent of the
Babylonian government. Jeremiah was the preacher in the
Holy City who continued to carry God's message to the
people. Perhaps Habakkuk and Zephaniah were contemporaries of his during those days of upheaval. An Egyptian
party constantly clamored for independence from Babylon
and insisted on going to Egypt for help. Jeremiah preached
submission to the king of Babylon as the only way to continue as a nation. He was very unpopular as a result of such
advice.

The end came for the kingdom of Judah in 587 B.C. when
Nebuchadrezzar returned to put down Zedekiah's rebellion
and take the rest of the people to join the exiles by the river
Chebar. It was a tragic hour for Jerusalem when the walls
were finally broken down, the houses burned, the Temple
destroyed and the people dragged away to captivity. Jere-

miah's prophecy was fulfilled and the wrath of God was poured out upon the rebellious sinners.

In Babylon (598-587 B.C.) conditions were just as deplorable. Daniel and a few other Jewish boys had been brought from Jerusalem in 605 B.C. Ezekiel and the upper class of the people were brought in 598 B.C. We must realize then that for eleven years these ten thousand exiles were living in a concentration camp in Babylon while Jeremiah and the home folk continued to carry on at Jerusalem. For five of these years the captives had no preacher to help them. Ezekiel began to serve as prophet in 593 B.C. and for six years he sought diligently to break down false hopes of an early return to Palestine and to prepare the captives for the tragic news of the destruction of Jerusalem.

The exiles lived by the Chebar canal, east of Babylon, the most beautiful city of the world. Palaces, gardens, temples and great fortifications made the city an outstanding show place of the East. The Jewish people, with Temple gone, national life gone, and very little opportunity for business, presented a pitiable picture. Writing came into its own. Rabbis, teachers, scribes and lecturers arose to lead the people in their discussions and inquiries. False prophets were plentiful. Complaints, murmurs and wails filled the air. Ezekiel calls the people *"rebellious, impudent, stiff-hearted, briers, thorns, scorpions."* (2:6.) To such an audience Ezekiel devoted the best years of his life.

THE MAN

An eminent scholar calls Ezekiel "the most influential man that we find in the whole course of Hebrew history." As a young man he was profoundly influenced by the preaching of Jeremiah and by the courageous reform attempted by Josiah. These two servants of Yahweh exerted a tremendous influence. Ezekiel was an aristocratic young descendant from Zadok's line. Even in the troublous days connected with the death of the Assyrian empire it was easy for him to maintain

his pride and confidence in the future of the priesthood of
Yahweh's chosen people.

When Jehoiachin surrendered to the invaders in 598 B.C.
the young prophet found himself in the midst of 10,000 captives on the way to the city of Babylon. For five years he lived
in exile without any thought of preaching. He perhaps
dreamed of the return to Jerusalem and the resumption of
his natural life among his friends.

His call. God laid His hand on him and called him to be
the prophet to the lonely exiles. In a dramatic fashion he
describes for us his vision and call to service. The holy Being
who appeared to him could go everywhere, had power in
every place, could see everything, and ruled the entire universe by His mighty hand. Very realistically Ezekiel was
ordered to "eat the roll" and then go forth as God's prophet.
He tells us that he came to the captives by the Chebar canal
with bitterness in his spirit. Fortunately he did not begin
preaching at once but sat down among them for seven days.
During these days his anger and bitterness left him and he
was able to understand the hearts of his people. He looked
at life through their window and saw something of the problems they were facing. We may be sure that he was a much
more effective preacher after this preparation. He knew more
about his congregation, understood them better, sympathized
with them, loved them and was able to help them much more
effectively. We do not wonder that he became such an effective pastor, teacher and preacher. He was God's man for an
hour of crisis.

His mission was clearly revealed to him by the indwelling
Spirit. He was to destroy false hopes of an early return to
Jerusalem, to interpret the meaning and purpose of the exile,
to gather up and preserve the teachings of historians, psalm-
ists and prophets, to organize new forms for the worship and
life in the restored community, to preserve Israel's soul in
Babylon, and to stimulate new hope for the future of Israel.
His task was to warn, exhort, console, allay fears, build up

hopes for the future, and act as an honest watchman during the dark days of captivity. So far as we can know the whole religious program was in his hands. When the other captives came in 587 B.C. his work was doubled. He probably served as God's watchman for about twenty-two years.

His method was unique. His vivid imagination, his dramatic style, his weird imagery, his peculiar psychic states, and his effectiveness in presenting truth, set him apart as an unusual prophet. In order to attract attention and drive home his message he cut his hair and beard with the sword and divided it in equal portions, drew pictures with vivid illustrations of a city's fall, dug a tunnel under the wall and dragged his possessions through after him while the people looked on in astonishment. In vivid language he described a visit to Jerusalem, carried by the hair of his head over mountain and plain, to investigate the evils of that wicked city. He used history as a text for his sermons and interpreted the text to the people. As a preacher, a writer, a pastor and a prophet of God, Ezekiel takes his place among the great men of the Old Testament. His peculiar nature was used of God to make a valuable contribution to the life of Israel in exile.

His character has already been partially pictured in these other discussions. In addition we may think of him as being strangely conscious of the hand of God upon him. He was never able to get away from that realization. It colored his whole philosophy and his utterances. He was utterly helpless before the mighty God who controlled him. He spent much time in meditation and deep thought. At times he was harsh, blunt and uncompromising. A man of deep convictions and fearless determination he was considered a strict moralist in an age when such men were not popular. At heart he was deeply sympathetic and had an abiding love for his people who needed a pastor. God used him mightily to work His will among the captives by the Chebar.

THE BOOK

Ezekiel's book gives evidence of careful planning and dating. It is orderly, systematic and well outlined. Oesterley and Robinson claim that Ezekiel preached in Jerusalem 602-597 B.C. and that chapters 1-24 were written during those years. It is not necessary to adopt such a theory in the light of all the available evidence. We believe that chapters 1-24 were written in Babylon during the years 593-587 B.C. and that chapters 25-48 were written after the fall of Jerusalem in 587 B.C.

It may be outlined as follows:

1-24   Certain doom for Jerusalem (593-587 B.C.)
  1-3   Vision and call
  4-24   Sins denounced
25-48   Hope for the future (587-571 B.C.)
  25-32   Seven surrounding nations denounced
  33-48   Israel to be restored and blessed
    33-39   Concerning the people
    40-48   Concerning worship in the new temple
      40-43   The temple
      44-46   Who may enter?
      47-48   Blessings for all

PREACHING VALUES

The book of Ezekiel is rich in spiritual truths that strike with peculiar force upon the hearts of men. In it we are brought face to face with a transcendent God, a self-existent being who has absolute power and is constantly revealed in glory. Since He rules over all peoples He is jealous of His own honor and rules with cold impartiality even when it causes dire suffering among men. In the richest passages He is pictured as genuinely concerned over the state of His people, willing to accept their repentance and reward them. He will see to it that men suffer for their sins but He is just as certain that full pardon and redemption will be theirs.

Ezekiel represents God as a seeking shepherd who will not rest until He has brought all His sheep into the fold.

God's full grace is the answer to man's need of salvation. He alone can put a new spirit in man. The old stony heart can be removed only by the divine hand. The Holy Spirit is to come to write the divine law on men's hearts.

Ezekiel's most distinctive doctrine is that of the moral responsibility of the individual soul. In a day when it was believed that a man had religion only as a member of the nation such a doctrine was strange and revolutionary. Jeremiah and Ezekiel taught that each individual had the right of personal fellowship with God. When the individual had such a right he must be prepared to accept the consequences of that privilege and stand on his own feet before an impartial judge. Neither guilt nor merit could be transferred to another. Farley says: "So strongly did Ezekiel feel this great responsibility that he could not be simply, like his predecessors, God's spokesman to the nation. He has a message to the individual. The prophet must needs become a pastor." [1]

Our Lord emphasized and beautified many of the truths which Ezekiel preached. Such truths as the efficacy of repentance, the value of the human soul, the tragic nature of sin as ingratitude, the need for a new heart, and the picture of the loving mercy of God forgiving any soul that comes in genuine repentance, found expression in the prophet of the Exile.

Some great passages.

> *I am about to send thee to the people of Israel . . .*
> *and thou shalt speak my words to them . . . Then*
> *the Spirit lifted me up and took me away and I*
> *went in bitterness, and the hand of Yahweh was*
> *heavy upon me. I came to the captives who were*

[1] *Ibid.*, p. 190.

*dwelling by the river Chebar . . . and I sat there
dumfounded among them for seven days.* (2:1-3:15.)

The call of Ezekiel to leave his comfortable home and go
to preach to the captives at Tel-Abib came as an unwelcome
interruption. He felt the hand of God upon him and realized
a divine compulsion that could not be resisted but he went
in bitterness of spirit to a distasteful task. Fortunately for
him and for the people he did not begin preaching immediately but sat among the distraught people for a whole week.
That experience gave him a clear understanding of their
problems, their miseries and their crying needs. The preacher
who is able to see life through the window of his people will
be able to help them and provide the leadership so sorely
needed. If husband and wife, father and son, pastor and
people, employer and employee could only adopt this prin-
ciple in dealing with each other much strife and bitterness
and pain could be avoided. It would result in increased
knowledge, a wider sympathy, a deeper love, a fuller joy, and
a more gracious helpfulness. Ezekiel was a great pastor with
the true shepherd heart.

*I have made thee a watchman . . . Give them warn-
ing from me. If thou givest him not warning . . .
his blood at thy hands I will require. Yet if thou
warn the wicked . . . thou hast saved thyself.*

(3:16-21.)

What a fearful responsibility God places on His watchmen!
How can we be indifferent and lazy and careless in the light
of these arresting words? If we believe them at all how can
we sleep or rest? Ezekiel heard the word of God lay the
burden of witnessing upon him. It said, "If you warn the
wicked—he may die in his sins but you have saved your own
soul. If you fail to warn him, his blood will be on your own
soul." What is our answer? How can we go about explaining
it away? Why not accept it as true and binding on us? (Cf.
33: 1-9 for a similar warning.)

I will give them one heart . . . a new spirit I will
put within them . . . they shall be my people . . .
I will be their God. (11:19, 20.)

Ezekiel follows Jeremiah in urging spiritual religion. It is
definitely a heart religion that God wants. The heart is beyond repair. A new one will be provided. Formalism must
be left behind. The spiritual emphasis will give them touch
with Yahweh that will transform their thinking, their worship, their conduct and their loyalty. A new spirit will be
their special gift from their God. (Cf. 18: 31; 36: 26 f.)

"The fathers have eaten sour grapes and the chil-
dren's teeth are set on edge." Behold all souls are
mine . . . The soul that sinneth, it shall die. Re-
turn ye, for why will ye die? For I have no pleasure
in the death of him who dies. (18:1-32.)

In this chapter personal religion finds rich expression.
Individual responsibility is presented with directness and
effectiveness. In 1-20 he declares that a man's standing before
God is not determined by *ancestry.* The grandfather (5-9)
is righteous and shall live. The son (10-13) chooses to be
unrighteous and shall die. The grandson (14-17) is righteous
and shall live. Heredity and ancestry need not bind a free
individual. In 21-29 he declares that a man's standing before
God is not determined by his own past conduct. God refuses
to act capriciously. Habit is no more omnipotent than heredity. In 30-32 Ezekiel appeals to the free individual to repent
and turn to a forgiving God. God is merciful, gracious, with
abundant mercy ready to grant a full pardon to the soul
that chooses to exercise his own free will and repent. The
volitional element is clearly emphasized. No man need be
bound by anything when he understands the free grace of
God and wants full pardon.

As I live, says the Lord Yahweh, I have no pleasure
in the death of the wicked; but that the wicked turn

from his way and live; turn ye, turn ye from your
evil ways, for why will ye die? (33:11.)

Yahweh takes an oath to emphasize his tremendous love
for men. He has been pictured as a cruel tryant who finds
pleasure in inflicting pain. Ezekiel discovers that He is a
merciful God who finds no pleasure in hurting or killing
but who loves all men with a tender, compassionate love. His
purpose includes a joyful welcome to those who return in
answer to His wooing call. The shepherd's pleasing question
seeks to awaken in the wanderer a desire to come home to
the Father's arms. That question is still one to send out to
wandering souls.

Woe to the shepherds that are feeding themselves!
. . . Ye eat . . . ye clothe you . . . ye kill . . . but the
flock ye feed not. My flock wandered . . . and there
was no one searching or seeking them. (34:2-6.)

A heart-rending picture is painted of the unfaithful
preachers of Ezekiel's day. The flock are scattered, untended
and hungry while selfish shepherds pamper themselves and
loll in idleness and luxury without any thought of their
responsibility. They are careful to look out for their own
food and clothing and comfort but no one else is to be considered for a minute. The true love of the shepherd is wholly
lacking for they could not behave in that way if they had the
right love for the sheep. No one was seeking them. Again
the prophet has driven his arrow deep into our heart. How
can we live in self-indulgence and selfishness while the lost
are wandering unsought? (Cf. also Jer. 23:1-8; Zech. 11:17;
Matt. 9:36; Mark 6:34; Jude 12.)

Behold I will search for my flock, and will seek
them out . . . I will deliver . . . I will bring . . . I
will gather . . . I will feed . . . The lost will I seek . . .
and I will bind up the injured . . . I will feed
them. (34:11-16.)

The true shepherd is here represented as being in love with his sheep and spending his days in search of them. Jesus must have had this passage in mind when He spoke of Himself as the *Good Shepherd*. Ezekiel saw Yahweh in the rôle of a seeking Shepherd with His whole being dedicated to the work of feeding the sheep. (Cf. also Ps. 23; John 10: 8, 11; Matt. 9: 36; 25: 32; Luke 19: 10; Heb. 13: 20; 1 Pet. 2:25.)

And he said to me, Son of man, can these bones live? . . . And I will put my Spirit in you, and ye shall live. (37:1-14.)

With weirdness, realism and dramatic force the prophet presents the heartening news that Israel may hope to live. A revival is possible! Even dry bones, without sinew and flesh and blood, can live. The coming of God's Spirit brings life. The same thrilling truth is still needed in a world that has dry bones everywhere. What we need is to have the Holy Spirit come with His quickening power that a genuine revival may sweep the earth. (Cf. also Gen. 2:7; Rev. 11: 11.)

These waters are streaming forth toward the eastern regions . . . and everything shall live whither the waters come . . . its fruit shall be for food and its leaf for healing. (47:1-12.)

The water of life is a favorite figure in the Old Testament. Desert areas need water that life may be possible. This stream which Ezekiel sees flowing from the Temple makes its way toward the arid regions of the Arabah. In an ever deepening stream it goes on its way to bring life and health and abundant fruit wherever it goes. It is the one remedy that is needed. Jesus took that figure as a basis for his sermon to the woman at the well. (Cf. also Ps. 1: 3; Ps. 46: 4; Joel 3: 18; Zech. 14: 8; John 4: 7-15; 7: 38; Rev. 22: 1, 2.)

PRACTICAL LESSONS OF PERMANENT VALUE

1. The heart of God yearns for the salvation of all men.
2. Each individual must bear the responsibility of his own sin.
3. The minister must not let personal griefs and disappointments injure his ministry.
4. The human will is more powerful in determining destiny than either heredity or environment.
5. The terrific responsibility that rests upon one of God's messengers should cause him to be faithful.
6. The proper emphasis should be placed on ritual if we expect right conduct and behavior.
7. Ezekiel helps us realize the efficacy of repentance and the reality of the atonement.
8. God would have us understand the full significance of His love expressed in the story of the Good Shepherd.
9. From God flows the life-giving stream that makes the heavenly healing possible for all men who will drink and live.
10. Before one can be effective as a teacher or preacher he must be able to see the problem from the other side as well as his own.

''' JONAH '''

WHAT DISCRIMINATING PREACHER HAS NOT WANTED TO DO something to help men see the rich treasures that lie buried behind an interpretation of Jonah that seeks only to make men laugh? Such a tragedy has held sway in the world all too long. May we turn our thoughts on the book to get the point of view that will make us love the divine message so that we may teach it intelligently.

How Interpret the Book?

1. The *mythical* interpretation. This view would present Jonah as pure fiction with an imaginary person and an imaginary experience.

2. The *allegorical* interpretation. (cf. Bunyan's *Pilgrim's Progress*). According to this view the story is a parable prepared for didactic purposes. Jonah is a human type of Israel. The fish represents Israel's captivity.

3. The *historical* interpretation. This view that the facts are true as recorded in the narrative, was held by both Jews and Christians until about one hundred years ago. The author of Tobit, the author of 3 Maccabees, and Josephus regarded it as literal history. Tobit warns his son (14:8) to flee from Nineveh because Jonah's prediction was still to be fulfilled. If it is not true as recorded the author placed a cruel stigma on a faithful preacher of the Lord, for there was a prophet in Israel by that name (II Kings 14:25).

The Times

We are told by the author of Kings that Jonah lived in the days of Jeroboam II. We know that this great ruler extended his borders from Hamath to the Dead Sea. While his own kingdom enjoyed ease, prosperity and peace the Syrians

186

were pushed back to their own land and other neighbors were weakened. Meanwhile Uzziah built up the same kind of kingdom in the South. Side by side these two vigorous kingdoms grew and prospered. Adad-nirari IV (810-782 B.C.) of Assyria made three trips to Palestine to keep his subjects in line but he did not molest Jeroboam.

It was in a day of unparalleled success and luxury that Jonah, the son of Amittai, did his preaching in Israel. The people of Israel were not disposed to think in friendly terms of any of the neighbors. An ugly, narrow, selfish nationalism had developed in their hearts. Israel was Yahweh's chosen people and they had fought bitter wars with all these neighbors. Not a single nation was exempt. Certainly no one in Israel had any love for the people of Nineveh.

The Man

Jonah, the son of Amittai, was probably born about four miles north of Nazareth. He was a popular preacher of good news for the kingdom (II Kings 14:25). Being a narrow patriot who loved his people and his land he found it difficult to understand and obey the call of God to go to Nineveh to announce the doom of that city so that the people might repent and live. Hating Assyria as he did, he sought escape by rebelling against the known will of the Lord. He was not a coward but a willful, strong, impulsive prophet who could not afford to let God make a serious mistake. He had an antisocial mind that could not see good come to the hated enemy. He feared God and yet ran from him and deliberately refused to be used in God's plan for a great city. He was a mighty preacher who showed unusual power in influencing those who heard his message.

The Book

The book is *about* Jonah rather than *by* him. There is no claim anywhere that the book was written by Jonah. It is a vivid narrative recounting the story of a prophet's willfulness and his subsequent behavior after God's correction. Farley says: "The Book of Jonah, then, like so many other parts of the O.T., is a parable, perhaps the greatest of O.T. parables, and that which comes nearest to the teaching of the greatest of all the parables of Jesus—the parable of the son who lost himself and was found. Whether, however, we regard the book as literal history or treat it as allegory, its purpose and meaning are evident, though if we regard it as a parable, its difficulties disappear. In either case the book becomes a most powerful appeal for foreign missions." [1]

It has been called "God's commentary on Obadiah." The Jews have esteemed it very highly. It has been chosen as the special portion of Scripture to be read on the sacred Day of Atonement. The great German scholar Cornill says of the book: "I cannot take up this marvelous book, or even speak of it, without the tears rising in my eyes."

Analysis of the book. Some one has given the following outline:

Chapter one, disobedience—running from God.
Chapter two, prayer—running to God.
Chapter three, preaching—running with God.
Chapter four, complaints—running ahead of God.

Another scheme has been suggested as follows:

1:1-3   disobedient
1:4-16   punished
1:17-2:10   preserved
3:1-4   preaching in Nineveh
3:5-10   conversion of the people
4:1-11   picture of a narrow prophet

Some pertinent comments. It will probably help the inquiring student to have a carefully selected appraisal from several men who have made a study of the Book of Jonah. Cadman says: "There is not a more modern book in the Old Testament than that of Jonah. Its ingenious mode of narration and dramatic strength are born of the religious imagina-

[1] *Ibid.*, p. 215.

tion in which it was composed. It sets forth as self-evident the truth that the Creator of the whole human family can know no distinction of race, creed or physical boundaries since all peoples are His offspring. . . . The prophet who wrote this document stretches forth a helping hand to all who love their fellow men." [2]

Ward says: "Over against the narrow prejudice of that early day, set the breadth of God's compassion and the profound mercy He proffers to the penitent. All men, whatever their time or clime, are His children. Their sin is God's sorrow, their salvation His concern. And the Book is intended to inculcate worthier views of God and man by removing the exclusiveness of Jewish thought, and the idea that grace was the sole possession of the covenant people." [3]

Cohon says: "The book is clearly an attack on the narrow, tribal Judaism of the day, and a plea for universality. God is one and mankind is one. Obviously to read the book of Jonah as history is to become involved in a mesh of highly embarrassing miracles and to pervert a great prophetic message into ludicrous nonsense. The book is Hebrew prophecy at its highest level, told in the form of a parable." [4]

Montefiore says: "It is the triumph of Judaism. The author of Jonah takes rank with the Second Isaiah as a master builder of Judaism. The one teaches the doctrine of absolute monotheism, the other the doctrine of human brotherhood to which the divine unity leads us on. The one lays down the nature of Israel's mission, the other illustrates it. Service and not privilege, or rather, the privilege of service; that is the reason of Israel's separateness and that is its justification." [5]

Gordon says: "The purest essence of Jewish liberalism is found, however, in the nobly conceived little book of Jonah,

---

[2] *Ibid.*, p. 182.
[3] *Ibid.*, p. 211.
[4] *Ibid.*, p. 219.
[5] *The Bible for Home Reading*, p. 419.

perhaps the most Christlike portion of the Old Testament." [6]

George Adam Smith says: "The truth which we find in the Book of Jonah is as full a revelation of God's will as prophecy anywhere achieves. That God has *granted to the Gentiles also repentance unto life is nowhere else in the Old Testament so vividly illustrated.* This lifts the teaching of the Book to equal rank with the second part of Isaiah, and nearest of our Twelve to the New Testament." [7]

Cornill says: "This apparently trivial book is one of the deepest and grandest that was ever written, and I should like to say to everyone that approaches it, 'Take off thy shoes, for the place whereon thou standest is holy ground.' In this book Israelitish prophecy quits the scene of battle as victor, and as victor in its severest struggle—that against itself." [8]

PRACTICAL LESSONS OF PERMANENT VALUE

1. The path of self-will is always downward.
2. In the hour of distress one turns to the God he has grieved.
3. How futile it is to resist the will of God!
4. In every heart there is an inherent capacity for God.
5. God knows and loves and seeks the salvation of all people.
6. One usually runs into a storm when he seeks to run away from God.
7. It is tragic to have to meet the storms of life without God's presence.
8. One tends to limit God by disobedience.
9. True repentance may avert the catastrophe that has been threatened.
10. No divinely given task may be lightly regarded.
11. It is utterly impossible to escape from God.
12. God would have us love all men as He loves them and give ourselves to the task of winning them.

[6] *Ibid.*, p. 348.
[7] *Ibid.*, p. 484.
[8] *Ibid.*, p. 457.

⁗ JOEL ⁗

THE NAME JOEL, OCCURRING FOURTEEN TIMES IN THE OLD
Testament, is compounded of two divine names, Jehovah
(Yahweh) and El, and means *Yahweh is God.* The prophet
lived and preached either in the days of Joash or during the
late days of the fourth century B.C. He spoke to Judah a message demanding repentance.

The Occasion. The people were faced with the most devastating plague of locusts that the land had known. Wave
after wave of these destroying pests had swept down upon
them. In addition a serious drought had come to complete
the picture of devastation and ruin. It was a tragic hour.
Men were desperate in their plight and ready to listen to
God's messenger as he interpreted the divine will. It was a
great hour for the preacher. Boldly, Joel faced the fright-
ened people with the divine call to repent.

The Date. Old Testament scholars are almost unanimous
in assigning a postexilic date to the prophecy of Joel. They
say that no mention is made of the Assyrians and Babylonians, the kings of Judah, the Northern Kingdom, or of the
"high places" (Bamoth). The word "Israel" is used for Judah,
the only sanctuary is at Jerusalem, the priest is the leader of
the sanctuary, the emphasis is mainly on the externals of
religion and the well-developed idea of the Day of Yahweh.
All these point to a late date for the composition of the book.
Likewise some linguistic peculiarities make it more than
probable that the language had been developing for many
centuries. They draw the definite conclusion that the book
was written after 432 B.C. The statement in 3:1-5

And I will hold judgment with them there
For my people and for my heritage Israel,

191

Whom they have scattered among the nations,
And my land they have divided.

seems to indicate that the Exile has already ended. It is significant, however, that its position in the Hebrew canon is between Hosea and Amos. If Joel lived in the postexilic period why was his book placed among the eighth century prophets? In the early part of Joash's reign the old priest Jehoiada was in active control of the government. He had just put down Athaliah with her religion of Baal. Since the boy Joash was not old enough to carry on the work of the kingdom, the entire load was upon the high priest. The consequent reform restored the worship of Yahweh in the land and returned the Temple to its place of prominence in the life of Israel. During these days conditions were the same as those pictured by Joel. This early date will account fully for the absence of all mention of Babylon, Assyria and Syria. In Joel the nations that are causing trouble are the Edomites, the Egyptians, the Philistines and the Phoenicians.

In addition to the suggestions already given, it seems reasonably certain that Amos quotes from Joel (3:16). In 1:2 Amos begins by carrying forward the work laid down by Joel. The idea of the *Day of Yahweh* was familiar to the people of Amos' day. They had become so familiar with it that they had misinterpreted its nature and implications. Amos was forced to set them right on that doctrine. Kirkpatrick says: "The positive arguments for the early date of Joel seems to me decidedly to preponderate, and the force of those for the late date diminishes upon examination . . . There is no sign of the apathy and neglect which Haggai and Zechariah rebuke, or of the contemptuous indifference which Malachi censures. . . . It is extremely difficult to see how Joel can be fitted into any part of the period after the Return without considerable assumptions." [1]

[1] *Ibid.*, p. 71.

THE BACKGROUND

If we accept the early date for the work of Joel, we think of Jerusalem under the control of the priests while a young boy is growing up to be a king. Athaliah, like her mother Jezebel, had destroyed the faith of God's people. Jehoiada was doing his best to rebuild a kingdom on godly principles. Jehu, the king in Israel, was working manfully to exterminate the last vestige of Jezebel's evil influence and the Baal worshipers who thronged the land. Elisha and his school of the prophets exerted a strong influence. Hazael, the cruel Syrian king, was fast becoming a terror to Israel and to all the surrounding kingdoms. Shalmanezer III of Assyria was still advancing in his drive to conquer the West. It was a trying period in the history of Palestine.

The locusts, the famine, the drought and the poverty that followed in the wake of these disasters prepared the minds of the people for thoughts about God. Fear of starvation brought them to the brink of despair only to reveal to them a God who had definite plans for them. He wanted His people to give Him a chance to prove His love.

THE MAN

We cannot know much about the prophet who wrote the book. We may be reasonably certain that he was a native of Jerusalem. He was a pious, godly, courageous preacher who came in the hour of opportunity to deliver the message of Yahweh to the chosen people. It is possible that he was a priest, since he shows such an intimate knowledge of the Temple and its worship programs. He had a distinct individuality and an original approach to the problems of his day. Clearly, directly and courageously he tackled the problem before him and suggested the divine remedy in terms that gripped the attention of his hearers. As a preacher of repentance he takes high rank among the prophets of God.

THE BOOK

The seventy-three verses of the book are written in rhythmical, elegant, impassioned style. Because of the freshness and excellence of the writing, it is clear that the book is either early or quite late. It is either quoted by, or quotes Isaiah, Amos, Micah, Nahum, Zephaniah, Obadiah, Ezekiel and Malachi.

The book falls into two equal divisions. In the first 37 verses (1:1-2:17) Joel speaks, calling the people to prayer and to repentance. In the second 36 verses (2:18-3:21) Yahweh speaks, promising to remove the plague, bestow prosperity, and give rich spiritual blessings.

Brice divides it as follows: [2]

1:1-2:11   *Devastation*. The sign of judgment.
2:12-17   *Supplication*. The call to repentance.
2:18-3:21   *Restoration*. The vision of blessing.

What are the interpretations of the locusts in 2:1-11?

1. *Allegorical* or *figurative*. This view would interpret the locusts as a symbol of the hostile armies of world powers that are to attack Israel in successive invasions.

2. *Apocalyptic*. This theory is that Joel uses the locusts as an apocalyptic device to give us an accurate description of the last days, when hosts of unearthly warriors shall come in battle array (as in Rev. 9).

3. *Actual* or *historical*. The locusts are real locusts that Joel sees swarming upon the vegetation of the land to devour it (cf. 2:4f.). Without doubt this third view is the correct one.

SOME GREAT VERSES

Hear this, ye old men, and give ear, all inhabitants in the land. (1:2.)

Joel was concerned lest the people of Jerusalem should miss the real meaning of the calamity. They faced utter ruin.

[2] *Ibid.*, pp. 13, 14.

Stark tragedy stared every one of them squarely in the face.
They were guilty of sin, and that sin must bring punishment.
He wanted them to see God's hand holding the rod and not
just the chastisement being inflicted. They could react in
several different ways to such suffering. Instead of self-pity,
cynical hardness, or stony indifference, he wanted them to
think themselves around to a genuine repentance that would
bring divine forgiveness.

> *Sanctify a fast, call a solemn assembly,*
> *Gather the old men and all the people of the land*
> *to the house of Yahweh your God and cry to Yah-*
> *weh.* (1:4.)

After the diagnosis had been made Joel quickly suggested
the remedy. Every person in the community was urged to
come together in humble recognition of Yahweh's hand in
the disaster. He challenged them to come to the solemn as-
sembly with a united prayer to God for mercy and deliverance. Fasting, prayer and penitence could be counted on to
bring God's forgiveness. An appalling crisis called for a sincere turning to God.

> *Turn to me with all your heart,*
> *And with fasting and with weeping,*
> *   and with mourning;*
> *And rend your hearts and not your garments,*
> *And turn unto Yahweh your God.*
> *For he is gracious and merciful*
> *Long-suffering and plenteous in mercy.* (2:12, 13.)

Joel challenged them to reality in prayer and repentance.
There was still time to turn back from their self-chosen
course of sin, and avert a more serious calamity that God was
sending upon them. The entire force of their moral purpose,
including intellect and affection, was to be turned Godward.
With genuine grief for sin they would come with weeping,
wailing and fasting to prostrate themselves before the com-

passionate God of love whom they had wounded. Driver says: "The prophet demands, for sin, a deeper grief still, one which should, speaking figuratively, *rend the hard and stony heart, and make it pervious to godlike thoughts and emotions. Compare the 'broken and crushed (contrite) heart' of Psalm 51:17."* [3] Yahweh's character (Exod. 34:6) is such that men may depend on His mercy when they have shown genuine repentance.

> *Then did the Lord become jealous for His land and*
> *He took pity on His people.* (2:18f.)

With these significant words Joel begins the second half of his book. We may imagine a definite break after 2:17 and a view of weeping, praying, repentant people on their faces before God. The prophet's work is finished. He merely recorded for us the Lord's answer to the prayers of His children. The locusts are to be destroyed, the gentle rains will come to refresh the cracked earth, the people will rejoice again in the renewal of God's favor. Joel is happy to report the fulfillment of all his assurances to them. Their God was ready to prove His eternal love.

> *And I will restore to you the years that the locust*
> *hath eaten, the cankerworm, and the caterpillar,*
> *and the palmerworm, my great army which I sent*
> *among you.* (2:25.)

Joel had a message of hope for the people in the hour of their darkest calamity. Repentance had brought them to the place where full restoration was possible. Ironsides says: "How striking the language, *My great army which I sent!* In the visitation referred to in chapter 1, they were in danger of beholding only the plague of locusts, and forgetting the One who sent it. He owns it as His army, which He had directed against the land for the discipline of His people. But in the coming day of the Lord, He will abundantly make up for all

[3] *Ibid.,* p. 57.

the loss of the past." [4] It is good to know that we have a God who can and will lift us and restore us to His own glorious presence again.

> *And after these things I will pour out my Spirit upon all flesh . . . and everyone who calls on the name of Yahweh will be saved.* (2:28, 32.)

The prophet of Pentecost followed his promises of material gifts with a glorious picture of spiritual blessings. The old and the young are to have that special anointing that will set them apart as the Lord's chosen instruments. They will have a clearer conception of divine truth and will be able to interpret God's will for the people. Even the slaves will be favored with this mysterious power. The universality of God's purpose is revealed as Joel opens the door to people of all lands and assures them that no bar will be erected against any one who calls on the name of the Lord. Peter claims the promise of Joel as not only fulfilled at Pentecost but as a fact yet to find richer fulfillment in God's own good time (Acts 2:17-21).

PRACTICAL LESSONS OF PERMANENT VALUE

1. The externals of religion are not to be lightly regarded (1:9, 13, 14; 2:12-17).
2. Disasters serve to turn men to God and prepare their minds to hear His voice.
3. An awakened sense of dependence upon God makes for a genuine religious experience.
4. Judgment is inevitable. No individual need hope for escape.
5. The character of the judgment day depends on the attitude of the heart. It may be a day of terror or a day of blessing.

[4] *Notes on the Minor Prophets*, p. 127.

6. Great calamities call for a nation-wide season of prayer and repentance.
7. The broken heart is the only sound heart.
8. Genuine repentance gives God a chance to send blessings instead of calamities.
9. God can "restore the years the locusts have eaten."
10. Sincere prayer brings the promise of Pentecost (2:28f; Num. 11:29; Acts 2:16f.)
11. God delights to include all men everywhere in His great gift of the Spirit.

‴ HAGGAI ‴·

THE WORLD SITS UP AND LISTENS WHEN A MAN COMES ALONG
who can challenge a nation to break away from habits that
have held them, and rise up to build a great temple for the
worship of their God. Haggai can well enlist the hearty
interest of all of us, for he was inspired of God to do the
impossible. He was able to produce the spark that set the
Jewish people to work to rebuild Yahweh's house.

THE TIMES

In 586 B.C. when Nebuchadrezzar captured Jerusalem, the
old Temple was completely destroyed. After fifty years in
Babylon the Jews were allowed the privilege of returning to
Jerusalem to rebuild the city and the ancient Temple. Cyrus
not only granted this privilege but supplied sufficient money
to guarantee the work.

Under Zerubbabel the people returned to the old home
and began carrying out Cyrus' orders. Eagerness and enthusiasm characterized the group as they cleared away the débris
and set up the foundations of the sacred building. Their
ardor was soon cooled, however, by the hostility of the
Samaritans and perhaps also by the hard labor that such
construction demanded. Each person became interested in
his own work and in the building of a private house. Nearly
sixteen years passed before Haggai came to call them to build
God's house. It is almost unbelievable that God's people
should have waited so long to do the very thing they came
back to see accomplished.

Cyrus, the great conqueror, was followed by his son Cambyses. The suicide of Cambyses in 522 B.C. precipitated the
land into a critical situation. Persia and Media with twenty
smaller groups broke away from the Empire. For a few

months a usurper claimed the throne. But gradually the mighty hand of Darius the Great gained control, and order grew out of chaos. His consolidation and organization of the empire so diverse in its elements was truly a monumental work. We may read the story of some of his exploits on the Behistun Rock.

During the days prior to the coming of Darius the Jewish people worked frantically to make a living and build their own houses. Poor crops, blasting, droughts, opposition of neighbors, failing trade, turmoil and misery, brought little comfort to the people who had come back to Jerusalem with such rosy dreams of a worthy·building for God. They were slaving and worrying but finding no genuine happiness. They were not even getting the things for which they were striving with such feverish anxiety. In the meantime God's house was still in ruins. Zerubbabel was the temporal ruler and Joshua was the high priest in charge of the worship of the people. These two chosen leaders seem not to have had any influence with the people in enlisting their aid to build the Lord's sanctuary. God's prophet must be called out to bring His word to governor, priest and people. Haggai and Zechariah stood side by side in this important task.

THE MAN

Very little is known of this patriotic Jewish layman who responded so enthusiastically to Yahweh's call. He was probably an old man (2:3) who had lived long in Babylon before coming to Jerusalem with the returning exiles. Some go so far as to claim that he had lived in Jerusalem before 586 B.C. His name is associated with Zechariah's as the author of certain psalms (Ps. 137 in the LXX; 14-148 in the LXX and the Peshitta; 111 in the Vulgate; 145 in the LXX, Peshitta, and the Vulgate). He loved the Temple devotedly and understood something of the loss the people were suffering without it. He had deep conviction that he was right, a blunt way of driving home the truth, and an assurance that he was going to have his way. In a plain and unadorned way he presented his message. There was a note of urgency that elicited rapt attention and instant obedience. Though neither an orator nor a poet he obtained results. Consciences were pricked, imaginations were stirred, the work was done. He was a man of one idea. God had set him on fire with a burning zeal. People were compelled to follow his orders. In some unseen way he was able to put godly courage into the hearts of his kinsmen and to inspire the vital enterprise.

Marcus Dods says: "It is never an easy task to persuade a whole population to make pecuniary sacrifices, to postpone private to public interests; and the probability is, that in these brief remains of the prophet Haggai, we have but one or two specimens of a ceaseless diligence and persistent determination which upheld and animated the whole people till the work was accomplished." [1]

Ward says: "Haggai was an accomplished craftsman. There is perhaps no other prophet that is more direct in his purpose, so pungent in his criticism, and yet so adept at reaching the object aimed at without obtruding either his methods or himself. He tips his arrows with scorn, wings them with sarcasm, and then speeds them skilfully to the mark. . . . His duty was to take the scattered embers of national pride and piety and, with his inspired breath, kindle the flame anew." [2]

Bewer says: "Haggai was strongly influenced by Ezekiel in his view of the importance of the temple for the new community and his fear of its profanation by foreigners, and like him he combined priestly and prophetic interests. He was no great prophet, but by his practical initiative he rendered a genuine service to his people. His eagerness and enthusiasm are still refreshing." [3]

Cadman says: "Haggai emerged from one of the low levels

[1] *Haggai, Zechariah, Malachi*, p. 46.
[2] *Ibid.*, pp. 283, 292.
[3] *Ibid.*, p. 235.

of the general discontent to tell his countrymen that the famine was Jehovah's penalty for their neglect of His honor. . . . In simple unpretentious ways the prophet endeavored to reanimate Judah's religious energies. He was a traditionalist rather than an original thinker and the influence of the priestly caste was evident in his homilies. . . . He lacked the stern and searching note of Jeremiah who had already declared that an undefiled faith was entirely independent of external supports. . . . He used the everyday language of a jaded people not to apologize for their dejection but to challenge it." [4]

Harrell says: "Haggai was not a man of spacious ideas such as characterized the ministry of Amos and Isaiah and Jeremiah. The occasion did not call for such a man, and God suits his prophets to the times. Haggai's greatness lies in this: he saw the duty next at hand and inspired his people to undertake it. He does not occupy a conspicuous place among the prophets, but he fills it as a man called and led of God." [5]

THE BOOK

The book is a collection of four brief articles written between the last week of August and the twenty-fourth day of December 520 B.C. Each oracle is specifically dated. One central purpose dominated the book. Haggai was determined to have the temple rebuilt and he went about persuading the people to begin the work.

The first oracle (1:2-11) is a word of rebuke and a call to action. The failure had been because of fear and selfishness. The ones who were holding back were men who lived in luxury. They were being punished because they had failed to honor Yahweh. They could not hope to enjoy the divine favor when they showed no concern for spiritual matters. The way to please God was to turn to Him and begin the actual work at once. The timber and the stones must be

[4] *Ibid.*, p. 130.
[5] *Ibid.*, p. 196.

brought so that the wrath of God might be lifted from them.

The historical interlude (1:12-15) describes the remarkable effect of this ringing challenge. Governor, priest and people began immediately to do the will of God. It was a pleasing response to an effective sermon.

The second oracle (2:1-9) was a call to courage and encouragement in the hour of disappointment. Some of the older ones were greatly disappointed when they saw that the new Temple would not measure up in splendor to the old Temple built by Solomon. These pessimists were dampening the enthusiasm of the builders. Haggai came from God with a revelation of His resources that were to be poured into this new structure. The Living God is to be in the midst of this new Temple and from it He will glorify Himself among the nations. God's eternal purpose is to bring more glory on His sanctuary. The eternal covenant still stood. They could depend on Yahweh to pour out His rich blessings upon them.

The third oracle (2:10-19) contains another appeal to conscience and in addition a call to patience. Haggai heard their complaints that the promised blessings were slow in coming although they had been working for three full months. He made it clear to them that the land had been defiled and profaned by their neglect. Pollution has a way of spreading far and deep. Evil manifests a power of infection more serious than holiness. Their sin could not be so easily and quickly expiated. Those years of selfishness, neglect and sin had rendered them unclean in God's sight. If they would persevere in the work and be faithful to their God they could be certain of victory. Fruitful seasons, good crops and rich blessings were to be theirs. The new day of fruitful gifts was dawning for them. (Zechariah was now preaching by his side.)

The fourth oracle (2:20-23) contains a message of hope to Zerubbabel who was to bask in the assurance that he was the chosen object of divine care and that he would be protected in the great overthrow that was to destroy surrounding nations.

He was to be the representative of Yahweh among the peoples of the earth. It was a glowing messianic promise that brought new hope to the discouraged people. In the hour of the fatal overthrow of surrounding nations this heir of David was to be safe as Yahweh's chosen signet. Let Israel resolve to endure all the hardships of the present in the assurance that better days await her.

PRACTICAL LESSONS OF PERMANENT VALUE

1. Difficult duties should be faced courageously and without delay.
2. A stern call to duty is a good tonic.
3. The God-given message will result in action.
4. We are not to live in fine dwellings and allow God's house to lie in ruins.
5. If material considerations crowd out God's house and worship our wealth costs too much.
6. How serious and lasting are the effects of evil (2:10-19)!
7. How futile is human effort and endeavor when separated from spiritual emphasis!
8. The best test of oratory is found in whether or not words stimulate action.
9. Full obedience to God is a necessary condition of approach to Him.
10. Outward splendor does not necessarily constitute true glory.
11. The book is a challenge to preachers to throw them-selves enthusiastically into a great program for God.

ʻʻʻ ZECHARIAH ʻʻʻ

IT IS A GREAT ACCOMPLISHMENT TO STAND ALONGSIDE AN AGED
Haggai and preach words of encouragement to people as they
drive themselves to hard labor toward the completion of a
difficult task. In those trying days from 520 B.C. to 516 B.C.
Zechariah proved his worth. His passionate enthusiasm for
the restoration of the Temple challenged the people to carry
on to the hour when the building was completed.

THE TIMES (See page 199)

Darius the Great found plenty of trouble when he came to
claim the throne of Persia at the death of Cambyses in 521
B.C. The great empire was made up of kingdoms and tribes
held together by the iron hands of Cyrus and his son. The
death of the king was a signal for uprisings in all parts of
the empire. At least nineteen important battles were fought
before Darius could take his place at the head of the group.
Then followed a reign of great prosperity that placed him
among the outstanding rulers of all history.

A serious depression, with crop failures and apparent ruin,
faced the Jewish people who had responded to the call of
Haggai to build the house of God. Under the pressure of
discouragement and want that faced them they found it easy
to fall out. The blunt, prosaic hammering that Haggai did
had its effect, but a new voice was needed to lift them into
the kind of enthusiasm that would keep them working to
the finish line. Zechariah came to the rescue to supply the
needed help. The two prophets did a significant work in
keeping the interest high and the hands working through all
the troublous days. It was a mighty undertaking carried on
under the most trying circumstances to its completion in 516
B.C.

The Man

Zechariah was probably a young preacher born in exile and brought to Jerusalem under the divine leadership for the specific task of helping to spur the builders to action. His name seems to mean *he whom Yahweh remembers*. His sensitive soul was strangely moved by the consciousness that God's house was still in ruins. When Haggai began preaching he could not restrain himself longer. Eagerly and with reckless abandon he threw himself into the work of helping his great friend. God had called him and the time was ripe for preaching. He did not hold back but gave his all in the proclamation of the message.

He does not rebuke or condemn or berate the people. With striking colors and vivid imagination he paints glowing pictures of the presence of God to strengthen and help. Words of inspiration flow from his lips. His hope for a new kingdom rests upon the faith he has in his own people to respond with willing hearts to the wishes of God. Obedience will bring rich blessings.

Ward says of him: "Buoyant and zealous, he had the soul of an artist and the eye of a seer. He made commonplace duty luminous with the light of his genius. He comforted men with thoughts of God's clemency and regard for the people of His choice. But he did even more—more than he could measure. He proclaimed the coming of that golden era when God's promises would be realized." [1]

Cadman says: "Zechariah's prophecy was not so much an emotional message as it was a literary product and as such comparable to a sacred drama of the Middle Ages. Its artistic merits were admirable but it lacked the regenerating strength of Hebrew prophecy at its apex." [2]

James says: "Zechariah was interested in building not only a temple to God but houses for people to live in. When he

[1] *Ibid.*, pp. 298, 306.
[2] *Ibid.*, p. 142.

talks of old people sitting in the sun and boys and girls playing in the streets; when he bids men to be strong and fear not, but build; when he welcomes all nations to God's house, then we understand him. He was very human and his influence made for humanity." [3]

Harrell says: "The oracles of Zechariah reflect a very engaging personality. He was imbued with the spirit and teachings of the prophets who had preceded him, and appeals to them as spokesmen of Jehovah. No prophet makes so large use of the Sacred Writings as he. He manifests a fondness for vision and symbol, and yet he does not permit his imagination to run riot. His leading ideas are simple and practical." [4]

THE BOOK

The book of Zechariah as we have it contains three sections: The first section (1-6) is made up of a series of visions designed to encourage the builders in their task. Both promises and warnings are found. The second section (7, 8) consists of a discourse on fasting designed to answer a special request from Bethel. Warning them against unethical formalism he urges them to perform deeds of practical righteousness. The third section (9-14) is a colorful unveiling of the future of Israel. God's shepherd is to be rejected and Israel must suffer severe tribulations but glorious days will come when Israel shall be restored to spiritual supremacy among the nations of the earth.

Brice states it as follows: [5]

1-6   Visions of Restoration
7, 8   Oracles of Appeal
9-14   Disclosures of Destiny

Chapters 1-6. These visions are definitely given to cheer the fainting workers and to make possible the completion of the building.

[3] *Ibid.,* p. 412.
[4] *Ibid.,* p. 197f.
[5] *Ibid.,* p. 120.

The opening appeal (1:1-6) is one of the strongest and most intensely spiritual calls to repentance found in the Old Testament. The people have not heeded the prophets and have failed to live according to the will of God. They may rest assured that the will of God abides and that the threatened judgments are coming true. Let them realize that the only way to have the favor of God upon them is to repent and obey the call of God.

The visions (1:7-6:8) came to impatient people who were tired and worn and skeptical as the promised blessings were slow in coming. God grants them these words of assurance and encouragement so that they may rise up and build.

1. THE HORSEMEN (1:7-17) (cf. Rev. 6:1-11). These four horsemen who have been doing patrol duty throughout the earth return to announce the assurance of peace and quiet because of God's presence.

2. THE FOUR HORNS and the FOUR SMITHS (1:18-21). Zechariah sees the four hostile powers that have scattered Israel beaten down and destroyed by four powers who are being used by Yahweh to save Israel. Brute force is to be put down.

3. THE MAN WITH THE MEASURING LINE (2:1-13). This vision declares that God will repeople, protect and dwell in the city of Jerusalem. The population will increase to the point that walls cannot surround them. They will not need walls of stone for Yahweh is to be a wall about His favorite city and a glory within the midst of His people.

4. JOSHUA ACCUSED BY THE ADVERSARY (3:1-10). He now turns from the city to the people. Joshua with soiled garments is a representative of the people. He is forgiven, cleansed, anointed, clothed in rich apparel and becomes the sign of the Messiah.

5. THE GOLDEN CHANDELIER AND THE TWO OLIVE TREES (4:1-14). This vision came as a distinct word of encouragement concerning Zerubbabel. He is truly God's anointed prince, endowed with power from God to do his work. God's two anointed leaders, Joshua and Zerubbabel, are the instru-

ments through whom the rich blessings are to come to the chosen people. The light of the Temple shall not burn out for it is *not by might nor by power* but by the living spirit of Yahweh that the victory will come.

6. THE FLYING ROLL (5:1-4). Before Israel can enjoy the rich blessings promised them they must be cleansed and purified. Spiritual reformation must precede temporal prosperity. Sinners and their sins must be purged from the land.

7. THE WOMAN IN THE EPHAH (5:5-11). Sin, personified as a woman, was seen sitting in a seven gallon measure as it was being transported to the land of Shinar. When the Temple is built evil must be removed from the land. These two visions imply the fulfillment of the promise in 3:9, *I will remove the iniquity of the land in one day.*

8. THE FOUR CHARIOTS (6:1-8). These powerful horses dashing in different directions represent the four winds of heaven under the direct control of Yahweh as He carries out His promises. The people may rest assured that every promise made will be fulfilled and that the guilty nations will be broken and that His people will rest in peace.

The coronation scene (6:9-15). From gold and silver recently received from Babylon they constructed a crown and placed it on the head of Joshua, the high priest. It was a definite prediction of the coming Messianic reign of peace and glory. The offices of the royal and the priestly were united in the Branch.

The question of authorship and date. Since 1632 scholars have been conscious of striking differences between chapters 1-8 and 9-14. It is quite generally admitted that the two sections of the book are by different authors. In chapters 1-8 the author speaks in the first person, the utterances are dated, the style is didactic instead of apocalyptic, almost every paragraph refers clearly to the events of the years 521-518 B.C., there are visions in which angels play a part. In chapters 9-14 the author's name is never mentioned, the first person is not used, the city is threatened with siege, no data for determining his age is given, the method is apocalyptic, there are no angels or visions mentioned and no reference to the building of the Temple.

We cannot hope to settle the matter but we can appreciate and use the book without question. If chapters 9-14 were written by Zechariah they were produced under circumstances far removed from the period around 520 B.C. He could have written them in his old age, under the guidance of the Holy Spirit, to describe the coming of the Messianic King. He prepared the road along which the celestial King was to ride in solemn grandeur.

DISTINCTIVE IDEAS

1. *A high regard for God's purpose* in the world. Zechariah was impressed with the part God's prophets had played in giving the divine message to the world. These prophets had died but the purpose of God was still unfulfilled and still clearly binding upon the people. God wanted his chosen representatives to repent and turn away from the wickedness that had destroyed their fathers. Zechariah was able to sense the meaning of God's will for his people. To him the Word of God was more than a storehouse of the facts of ancient history. It was for him an ever-present witness to the living presence of God in human experience. God's purpose is to help men, and toward that end He will continue His efforts.

2. *The world-wide reach of God's kingdom* (2:11; 6:15; 8:23; 14:16). Zechariah caught something of the spirit of the great prophet to the exiles and predicted the full growth and extent of the kingdom. Instead of a city built on the old foundations and a religion corresponding exactly to the pre-exilic pattern he conceived the plan of God as embracing a multitude of people and having as its central purpose a spiritual religion that could influence individuals to be like Him in thought, word and deed. The city is not to be an armed fortress with guns and engines of war as its defense but a

garden city completely filled with peaceful men, women and children.

3. *The coming Messiah* (2:10f.; 3:8f.; 6:12f.; 9:9-17; 11:4-14; 12:10; 13:7-9; 14:8f.) Zechariah's picture of the coming Messiah stirs the soul. This great King is to come as the Prince of peace (9:9, 10) *vindicated, victorious* and *lowly.* He comes triumphantly and yet in the guise of peace. Instead of riding a war horse he rides a humble beast used by kings and notables on missions of peace.

Such expressions as: *they weighed for my price thirty pieces of silver, and I took the thirty pieces of silver, and cast them to the potter in the house of the Lord; I was wounded in the house of my friends; He that eateth bread with me hath lifted up his hand against me; they shall look upon me whom they have pierced; I will smite the shepherd and the sheep shall be scattered,* and the references to the Messianic King and the Good Shepherd point forward to the life and ministry and death of our Lord.

4. *The divine sovereignty* (14:7-11). Finally the great conflict will end in a glorious victory for Israel. The temporary victory gained by the enemies of God will be forgotten when the Messiah in all His might shall put all enemies under His feet and establish His kingdom in Jerusalem. As the capital Zion shall then be the holy city of God. *At evening time there shall be light.*

Practical Lessons of Permanent Value

1. Dynamic preaching has peculiar power to restore drooping faith.

2. God will restore the stream of blessings on people who build His house.

3. The true glory of a city is to be found in its devotion to the living God.

4. The pastor still may hear the challenge of God to *feed, guide* and *guard* the flock.

5. For the godly soul there is joy in knowing that *at evening time there shall be light.*

6. Fasting and mourning are utterly useless unless the heart is pouring itself out to God.

7. A house of worship is necessary for the proper development of spiritual religion.

8. In God's plan true religion is destined to become universal.

9. It is important for God's followers to maintain a hopeful, optimistic outlook—knowing that He cannot fail.

10. Zechariah had a remarkable ideal for his city: *Jerusalem shall be called the city of truth.*

''' MALACHI '''

Again we face a man of God who has sensed the futility of the cold, formal, external type of religion that masquerades under the name of the genuine. In dynamic fashion he rebels and throws all that he can muster into the work of bringing the people back to the spiritual conception of worship that God requires. In his courageous attack on the priests he proves himself a hero. The course of his sharp arraignment reveals clearly the divine ideal for men who have been chosen as God's servants.

The Times

Almost nothing is known of the little community at Jerusalem from the dedication of the Temple in 516 B.C. to the coming of Nehemiah in 445 B.C. For more than sixty years the books are closed and the records are silent. Ezra came from Babylon with some new recruits in the year 458 B.C. but very little information is given concerning the people. Darius continued his significant career as king of the Persian Empire from 521 B.C. to 485 B.C. He was followed by Xerxes from 485 B.C. to 465 B.C. His son Artaxerxes reigned from 465 B.C. to 435 B.C. It was during these years that the Persians locked horns with the Greeks for the supremacy of the world. In 490 B.C. the Greek leader Miltiades defeated the Persians on the plains of Marathon in one of the decisive battles of the world. In 480 B.C. the Greeks made their memorable stand at Thermopylae and the mighty Persian fleet was destroyed at Salamis. Xerxes lost Europe and the flower of his army at Plataea the next year. It was the beginning of the golden age of Greek culture. Pericles was born the year Marathon was fought. Socrates was born twenty years later.

The Roman Republic was founded in 509 B.C. Europe was ready to succeed Asia as the arbiter of world affairs.

In Jerusalem the situation was grave. The fair promises uttered by the great prophet of the Exile and by Zechariah had failed to materialize. The people had become increasingly indifferent to spiritual matters. No prophet arose to interpret the will of God to them. Religion lost its glow and people became cynical, skeptical and godless. The coming of Ezra, the brilliant young scribe, from the Persian capital, bringing with him many of the rolls of Scripture, failed to bring them back to the high place they had enjoyed.

In 445 B.C. *Nehemiah,* a valued member of the court of Artaxerxes, was sent to Jerusalem to rebuild the walls that had been in ruins since 587 B.C. when the city was destroyed by Nebuchadrezzar. In spite of vicious opposition the walls were completed and the city was made safe from attack. Meanwhile Nehemiah had welded the people into a strong group who held him in high esteem and stood ready to obey his commands. As governor of the city he was able to effect sweeping reforms. It seems that he returned to the Persian court in 433 B.C. but came back to Jerusalem after a year.

The people were in the midst of a serious economic depression. Crops were poor, parasites ruined the plants, the fruit was disappointing. The priests were so corrupt and immoral that a spirit of skepticism pervaded the entire population. The people complained against God, bemoaned their sad plight, refused to pay their tithes and offerings, were guilty of social injustice, and had mixed themselves with the heathen people of the land. Divorce was common, Yahweh's covenant had been forgotten, and a low type of behavior was the common order of the day. Alliances had been formed with their neighbors so that they might have economic salvation but it had involved them in tragic consequences. Worship had degenerated into empty and indecent formalism. The nobles of the land who wanted the profit from religion without being willing to pay the cost, caused the serious trouble. The example and conduct of the nobles and the priests affected the whole community. Everybody was disposed to question the authority and the method of God. It was a serious situation that called for a fearless servant of God. Malachi was God's man for the crisis.

THE MAN

Malachi was a fearless reformer who spoke directly to the sinners of his day without hesitation or embarrassment. The name means "my messenger" and might be merely an editorial note taken from 3:1 in the absence of information concerning the author. We know that by the second century it was regarded as a proper name. The Targum assigned the book to Ezra. The LXX says: "An oracle of the hand of the Lord against Israel by the hand of his messenger." We may never know whether the word "Malachi" is a proper name or whether it is merely taken over as a name. We do know that it is a very suitable name and that there is no real argument against it. If the name was his it was probably given him at the time of his call to the prophetic office. Fortunately the identity of the author is not so essential for the authentication of his message.

We may rest assured that he was a strong, vigorous, clearcut personality who was strongly opposed to any person who treated the Temple and the things of the Spirit with indifference and carelessness. He was on fire with spiritual zeal to bring about the sort of reform that would guarantee justice and right for all the people and bring them to worship Yahweh as their own loving God. Perhaps Nehemiah influenced him to put forth such strong efforts on behalf of righteousness and godliness. It is probably best to place him in the period during Nehemiah's return to the Persian court, where he served as a strong ally in the vigorous reforms instituted by Ezra and Nehemiah.

Harrell says: "His book is the discerning analysis of a teacher rather than the impassioned appeal of an evangelist.

Through it speaks one who is keenly sensitive to the sordidness and negligence of his people."[1]

Ward says: "If he lacked the originality and insight of some of the former prophets, he certainly possessed power to enter the lists with evil, and to wrestle against entrenched abuses. Undismayed by his adversaries, with indomitable bravery Malachi girded himself for what the hour might bring forth. He feared no man because he feared God so much. With rapier thrust, he struck home. Skilfully he stripped off the hypocritical vesture with which priestly hands had decked the skeleton of wickedness."[2]

Farrar describes Malachi as "the last flush in the sunset of Hebrew prophecy. He is like a late evening which brings a long day to a close, but he is also like a morning dawn which brings with it the promise of a new and more glorious day."[3]

Cohon says: "To the bragging skeptics of his day Malachi addressed himself with a reaffirmation of his faith in a just God. In his book of remembrance he has inscribed the faithful, and the day will come when the righteousness will be separated from the wicked. 'Malachi' was probably not the real name of the prophet. It is eminently fitting that such an appellation be given to the man whose words complete the canon of biblical prophecy."[4]

Smith says: "The author of Malachi sets himself to the task of encouraging his people and of quickening their faith. He recognizes clearly the state of mind of his contemporaries, and meets them on their own level. He himself is full of courage and enthusiasm, and is dominated by an invincible faith. These attitudes he seeks to awaken in the minds and hearts of his people."[5]

---

[1] *Ibid.*, p. 205.
[2] *Ibid.*, p. 327.
[3] Quoted by Farley, p. 275.
[4] *Ibid.*, p. 212.
[5] *Ibid.*, p. 215.

THE BOOK

Malachi's book differs greatly from the other prophetical treatises. He does not present certain independent sermons or addresses but launches into an argument with his contemporaries. We can see and hear the audience respond to his open-air preaching with comments, questions, objections and excuses. The master debater takes each objection and answers it before going forward with another. Priest and people are charged with specific crimes while the weak replies continue to come back at him. Throughout the entire dialogue he is describing the divine love, revealing the faithlessness and ingratitude of the people, calling for genuine repentance, answering the skeptics, challenging the current godlessness and making glorious promises for those who are faithful.

In 1:1-2:9 he pictures the fullness of Yahweh's love for Israel. In 2:17-4:6 he discusses the divine equity. Against people who deny both the love and the justice of God he sets himself in strong argument.

To those who doubted God's love he points out the numerous special privileges that they enjoy. Other nations lay in ruins while Judah enjoyed the rich blessings of God. Such love and care should call forth gratitude and joyous service. Instead they have shown open contempt for the Temple and for the ritual requirements of God. The priests have led the people astray. They should have been teachers of the people (2:7). God wanted more than personal sanctity. He needed competent and trustworthy interpreters of the Word to ignorant people. It was a terrific arraignment of chosen representatives of God. They have actually led the people astray and as false leaders of the blind they have become contemptible in the eyes of God and men.

When men complained that their offerings were not accepted at the altar, Malachi reminded them that a holy God cannot be expected to accept offerings from the hand of those who were living sinful lives and who were guilty of divorcing their wives to marry heathen women. In God's sight it was an abominable practice. One living in open and willful sin could not expect God's smile upon his sacrifices. Malachi sensed something of the divine love for the home and the sacred tie of the marriage bond.

They were guilty of robbing God of the love and loyalty that was due him. That love and loyalty should have issued in a life of beautiful service. They had therefore robbed God of more than they realized. It was a terrific charge. The charge was followed by some serious threats. Such behavior and such attitudes must bring down upon them serious consequences. God would purge, cleanse, rebuke and punish His people.

The exhortations to come back to God by way of sincere repentance involved several things. They must quit robbing God. God's house and God's worship must be supported. The tithes and the offerings must be brought to the holy sanctuary. The hearts must be right so that prayers might rise from clean lips. God is ready and anxious to be put to the test by honest seekers after divine gifts. The windows of heaven have been closed too long. An abundant supply of rich blessings are ready to pour out at the first call of hearts that begin to love God again. The prophet continues to promise rich blessings for all who will return to God in genuine repentance. It will be a new day for God's people.

Practical Lessons of Permanent Value

1. God loves a pure, clean, happy home.
2. Divorce is an abomination in his sight.
3. Insincerity in worship is an insult to God.
4. God's people should be zealous for the honor of His sanctuary.
5. Impatience often leads to a false accusation of God.
6. One who lives in willful sin cannot hope to please God by costly sacrifices.

7. Carelessness and indifference in worship may be the first step in spiritual decline.
8. Laxity in the externals of worship is an indication of spiritual apathy.
9. Carelessness in worship and looseness in living blunt man's moral appreciations.
10. Spiritual temperature can be judged by our response to God's requirements on giving.
11. The low ideals of God's priests affect the people in the pew.
12. When God's minister fails to study and teach truth and morals the people suffer.
13. Cheap religion avails nothing, and sacrifices grudgingly given are displeasing to God.
14. Each man may determine for himself whether the *Day of Yahweh* is to be a day of terror or a day of joy.
15. God still holds out the challenge to all his chosen ones to put him to the test to find the rich supply of blessings that are available.
16. Instead of airing our doubts to others we may speak in secret to God about our doubts, so that He may guide us into truth and peace.

INDEX OF NAMES AND PLACES

The names of the Prophets discussed in this book are not listed in the Index. Consult the Table of Contents.

INDEX OF SCRIPTURE REFERENCES